KV-549-724

STAR WARS™
GALAXY GUIDE

Native blaster emits bolts of kinetic force

Mustafarian gas mask with flare-guard goggles

Life-support pack

Insulated fabric

Armor made from discarded lava flea shells

Weapon controls

Dense skirt protects legs

Heat-resistant boots

MUSTAFARIAN

Contents

Motion/sound
sensor system

Macrobinocular
viewplate

Utility pouch

Knee-pad
rocket dart
launchers

Reinforced
double-layered
flight suit

BOBA FETT

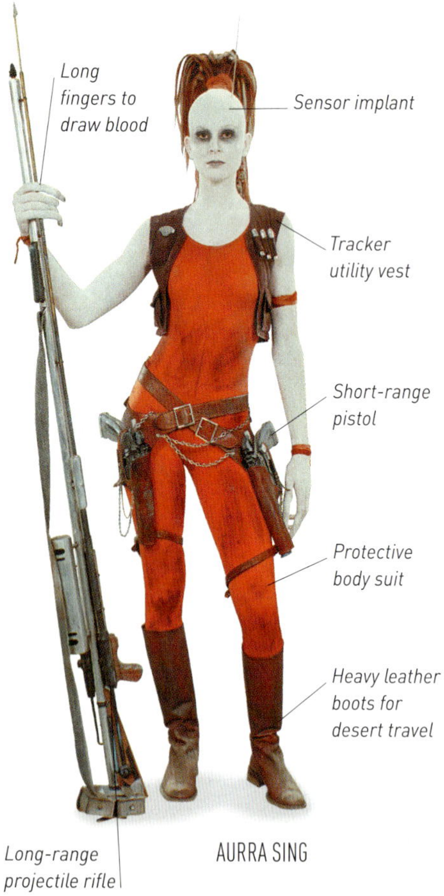

Long
fingers to
draw blood

Sensor implant

Tracker
utility vest

Short-range
pistol

Protective
body suit

Heavy leather
boots for
desert travel

Long-range
projectile rifle

AURRA SING

STAR WARS

GALAXY GUIDE

Field generator
confines bird

Optional data-feed
package

Full-readout display

PODRACE FAN'S
MACROBINOCULARS

Display crest

Engineer's name,
"Jabesq," in
Naboo Futhork

Pylat bird

NEIMOIDIAN
BIRD CAGE

Sound-damping
layers

NABOO HANGAR CHIEF
ENGINEER'S HELMET

Manual start
knob

Heat radiator
shroud

Simple ionizer
array

Complex
ionizer array

Sand-tight
construction

Display confirms
transmission of
door entry code

TATOOINE GUNMAN'S BLASTER

GYRDA KEYPAD

Charge generator
assembly

Sweeper screen stabilizes
local fields for delicate
maintenance

Antenna for
communication
with Theed Palace
computer system

Spinner motor

Cooling
unit

HANGAR DECK
SCRUBBER DROID

Stereo sniffers
find drops of
dangerous
leaked fuel

WATTO'S IONIZER

Sunshield
fabric

MOS ESPA COOLTH BACKPACK

Monocular navigation
photoreceptor

Fuel scrubbers
(on underside)

Cycling field generators

JEDI LIGHTSABER

EPISODE I
THE PHANTOM MENACE

EPISODE I travels back to the beginning of the *Star Wars* saga, a generation before Luke Skywalker meets Ben Kenobi and sets out on his path to destiny. In this era, Luke Skywalker's father Anakin is nine years old, and the great free Galactic Republic still stands, although its power is starting to falter. This time is populated with new characters, whose worlds are replete with gleaming spacecraft, intricate clothing, and exotic-looking robots. Just as in the real world, these artifacts tell a story. They are clues to identity. From the deathly pale appearance of Trade Federation battle droids to the tasty gorgs of Mos Espa marketplace and the fangs of the colo claw fish, the Visual Dictionary is your guide to the dazzling worlds explored in this first episode of the *Star Wars* fantasy. Because even at the beginning, there's a lot to catch up on. So jump on board.

And brace yourself.

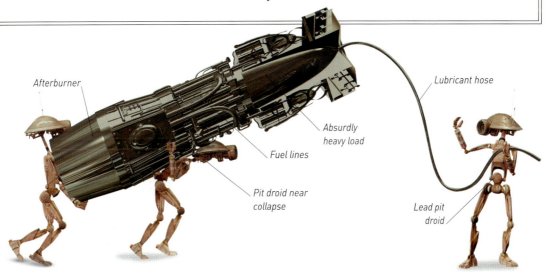

Afterburner

Lubricant hose

Absurdly heavy load

Fuel lines

Pit droid near collapse

Lead pit droid

Emitter assembly

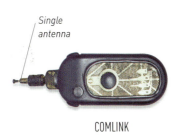

Single antenna

COMLINK

BLISSL TUNER
(MUSICAL INSTRUMENT)

SLAVE QUARTERS
BRAZIER

Hooded cloak

Hidden visage

Sith clasp

The Phantom Menace

FOUNDED LONG AGO, the Republic has united countless thousands of star systems under a single, far-reaching government. In millennia past, great sections of the Republic fought each other even as they clung to threads of unity. Peace and justice came to prevail under the protection of the wise and powerful Jedi, who draw on a mystical power known as the Force. Through the guidance of the Galactic Senate, civilization grew and the Republic became prosperous. But the price of comfort was weakness. The institutions of government became decadent and Jedi numbers dwindled to a mere ten thousand. Now, the Force itself is unbalanced and great change seems imminent...

Coruscant

A world enveloped in a single city, Coruscant is the home of galactic government and the effective center of the known universe. Representatives from all member worlds congregate here to participate in the colossal enterprise of galactic government. From among the thousands within the senate chamber, the pleas of a single voice must be heard to save the small planet of Naboo from invasion.

On Coruscant, the leadership of the Galactic Senate is served by the Jedi—guardians of peace and justice in the Galaxy. It is on the decisions and actions of the Jedi High Council that the fate of the galaxy will turn as the forces of darkness begin to gather their strength.

Darth Sidious

The Sith Lord Darth Sidious sets into motion the final stages of his order's 2,000-year-old plan to destroy the Jedi. Working patiently, Sidious has extended his power and influence deep into the galactic government. Using his grasp of psychology and bureaucracy to stifle justice, he brings about the crisis he needs to make his move for domination.

Coruscant provides a hiding place for the mysterious Sith. This ancient dark order has been waiting in the shadows, preparing to prey upon the Galactic Republic's time of weakness and usher in a new era of Sith rule. This phantom menace radiates outward from the center, drawing into its web individuals and worlds that lie far beyond Coruscant.

Theed Royal Palace | Palace forecourt | Naboo philosophers

Naboo

The provincial and little-populated planet of Naboo has benefited greatly from membership in the Republic. Within an idyll of serenity, Naboo decorative architecture expresses the planet's philosophy of arts and a harmonious way of life. The Naboo have come to regard their privilege as a birthright, and do not realize the extent to which they are dependent on the core strength of galactic government to protect them. Only when crisis descends will they face the frightening realization that the only strength they can depend on is their own.

Expressive of Naboo style in its glistening silver finish and dreamlike, artful contours, the Royal Starship is nonetheless built around a core of foreign-made engine systems. Naboo society is similarly dependent on outside industry.

Hydrostatic bubbles keep out water

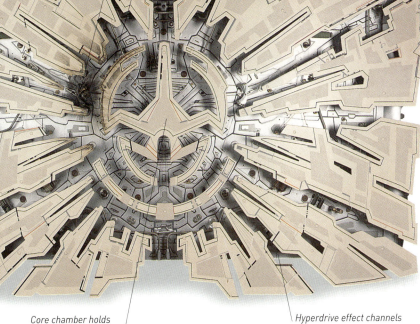

Overload burnout scar   *Area of field leakage*   *Naboo-made charge planes*   *Gungan-style artistic floor pattern*

Core chamber holds Nubian T-14 generator

Hyperdrive effect channels improve supralight performance

Otoh Gunga

Removed from outside contact, the underwater Gungan cities of Naboo glisten like scintillating jewelry. The Gungan capital city, Otoh Gunga, prides itself on being independent of foreign influences. Nonetheless, it relies upon a quiet but vital trade with the Naboo. In this, as in the danger they face from the Trade Federation, the Gungans find that they are more connected with outsiders than they confess.

Typical Gungan design

Hyperdrive Core

A dazzling example of Naboo style, the hyperdrive core of the Royal Starship is an intricate maze of charge planes and effect channels that allows the ship to slip smoothly beyond lightspeed. When the Nubian-made generator inside the core fails under the energy overloads encountered in battle, the Naboo begin to learn the realities of their dependence on the outside world.

TOUCHDOWN ON TATOOINE
The Naboo Royal Starship is forced by the broken hyperdrive core to land on the desert world of Tatooine. Queen Amidala must seek refuge in this wilderness and stake her hopes on desperate chance.

Slave quarters   Rough adobe walls

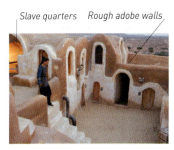

Tatooine

Beyond the reach of the Republic are the worlds of the Outer Rim, a frontier where extremes of freedom and slavery coexist. Tatooine is ruled by wealthy trading barons and gangsters. The adobe architecture of Mos Espa looks as rugged and primitive as the planet itself, but the thick walls hide sophisticated interior cooling systems. On Tatooine, not everything is what it seems—as those aboard the Naboo Royal Starship find when they encounter a slave boy named Anakin Skywalker.

Mace Windu
WISE NEGOTIATOR

SENIOR MEMBER of the Jedi Council, Mace Windu's wisdom and self-sacrifice is legendary. In a long and adventurous career, he has repeatedly risked his life to resolve great conflicts in fairness to both sides. Windu is sober and cool-minded but is also capable of dramatic actions in the face of danger. Always ready to risk himself, Mace Windu is very reluctant to risk the lives of others. In particular, he is wary of fellow Jedi Qui-Gon Jinn's headstrong belief in Anakin Skywalker, and senses great danger in the boy. These concerns weigh heavily upon him as he considers them against his friendship and respect for Qui-Gon.

Time and again, Mace Windu has stood at the center of great conflicts. His fame has only added to his negotiating skills.

Under-tunic

Tunic

Jedi robe

Deflector shield generator

Crew lounge

Color indicates diplomatic status

Lightsaber

Utility belt

Docking ring

Cockpit

Republic Cruiser

Jedi, diplomats, and ambassadors travel to trouble spots around the galaxy aboard the Republic Cruiser. This vessel's striking red color declares its political neutrality. In its well-armored salon pods, high-level negotiations take place between factions in conflict.

Diplomatic salon pod

The Jedi High Council is secretly called upon by Supreme Chancellor Valorum of the Galactic Senate to settle the conflict with the Trade Federation. Mace Windu summons a pair of his most able Jedi for the mission. Windu little suspects the evil and danger awaiting Jedi Master Qui-Gon Jinn and his apprentice Obi-Wan Kenobi within the Trade Federation fleet.

Blade projection plate

Blade modulation circuitry

Handgrip ridges

Activator

Blade length adjust

Radiator casing segment

DATA FILE

> The Jedi use the lightsaber as a symbol of their dedication to combat in defense, not attack, and of their philosophical concern for finely tuned mind and body skills.

> Ambassadors, mediators, and counselors, Jedi are warriors only as a last resort.

MACE WINDU'S LIGHTSABER

Yoda
ANCIENT MASTER

WELL INTO HIS 800s, Yoda is the oldest member of the Jedi High Council, as well as its most deeply perceptive Master. A great traveler in his younger years, Yoda has visited hundreds of worlds on his own, spending years learning different lifeways and appreciating the infinitely variable nuances of the Force. Yoda takes a personal interest in the progress of Qui-Gon Jinn and his apprentice Obi-Wan Kenobi. Yoda recognizes their strength and potential even as he disagrees with some of their "dangerously reckless" choices.

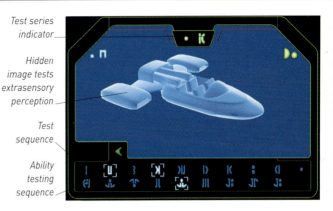

Test series indicator

Hidden image tests extrasensory perception

Test sequence

Ability testing sequence

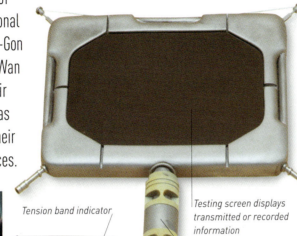

Testing Screen

The Jedi High Council uses multi-function viewscreens to test Jedi apprentices. These screens are built without buttons and are operated by Jedi mind powers. Only Force-attuned individuals can follow the high-speed series of images generated on screen. Testing screens keep the Jedi Council members in constant practice with their Force abilities.

Blade emitter shroud

Activator matrix

YODA'S LIGHTSABER

Testing screen displays transmitted or recorded information

Control probe

Standard tests stored in memory cell

Handgrip

Test results are recorded in removable memory cell

Sensitive ears

Custom-made Council seat

Well-worn Jedi robe

The Jedi draw their power from the Force, an omnipresent, subtle energy field surrounding all living things. The Force can lend telekinetic powers and give insights into the future, the past, or the thoughts of others.

Tension band indicator

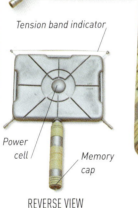

Power cell

Memory cap

REVERSE VIEW

Having seen so much of life, Yoda views all that happens with a long perspective. Less active now than in his younger years, Yoda remains one of the two most important voices of wisdom on the Jedi High Council along with Mace Windu.

DATA FILE

> Yoda's gimer stick cane helps him walk long distances and has natural plant substances that aid meditation when chewed.

> It has been many years since Yoda has needed to wield his special lightsaber. Yoda takes quiet satisfaction in finding nonviolent solutions.

The Jedi High Council

THE TWELVE MEMBERS of the Jedi High Council represent a gathering of great minds who have proven themselves and their abilities in the service of peace and justice. Confident in their attunement to the Force, the Council members work together in trust, free from the petty constraints of ego and jealousy. Their Council Chamber is a place of open thought and speech, a realm of mutual respect, and a haven of shared noble purpose. The Council is composed of five permanent members who have accepted a lifetime commitment to the difficult work of the Jedi. In addition, four long-term members serve until they choose to step down and three limited-term members sit for specified terms. This balance of membership keeps the Council wise and vigorous.

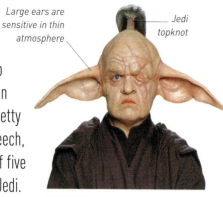

Large ears are sensitive in thin atmosphere

Jedi topknot

EVEN PIELL
Jedi Master Even Piell bears a scar across his eye as a grisly trophy of a victory against terrorists who made the mistake of underestimating the diminutive Jedi Master.

The Council Chamber is located atop the central spire of the Jedi Temple on the galactic capital planet, Coruscant. The 12 members sit in a ring of chairs that are spaced equally around the chamber.

Yarael Poof

The attenuated Quermian Yarael Poof is the consummate master of Jedi mind tricks. He uses Force suggestions to bring conflicts to an abrupt end, turning combatants' own fears against themselves.

Quermian upper brain

Quermians are noseless as they smell with olfactory organs in their hands

Long neck for peering above low vegetation mats

Robe hides second set of arms and chest with lower brain

Traditional Quermian cannom collar

Well-developed horns

Customary humanoid Jedi robes

Saesee Tiin

Tough skin impervious to high winds of Iktotchon

An Iktotchi pilot, Saesee Tiin is best able to focus while traveling at extremely high speeds—at the controls of the finest spacecraft. He offers a unique perspective on the Council as his telepathic mind is always racing ahead to foresee possibilities.

Large brain supported by second heart

Surcoat adapted from ancient Cerean garb

Lightsaber

Cerean cuffs

Plain trousers

Ki-Adi-Mundi

A Jedi Knight from the largely unspoiled paradise world of Cerea, Ki-Adi-Mundi's high-domed head holds a complex binary brain. Recently added to the Council, Ki-Adi-Mundi has not yet taken a Padawan learner.

Vestigial horn patterns identify races of Iridonian Zabrak

Tholoth headdress

EETH KOTH
Iridonian Zabrak such as Eeth Koth are renowned for their mental discipline, which allows them to tolerate great physical suffering. This ability is born of surviving their harsh homeworld.

Dense hair deters biting cygnats of Thisspias

Utility pouch

OPPO RANCISIS
Abdicating his throne on Thisspias, Oppo Rancisis instead sought to serve the entire galaxy among the Jedi order based on Coruscant. When negotiations fail, Rancisis ensures that Jedi-counseled military tactics are cunning and effective.

Mark of illumination

Tall travel boots

DEPA BILLABA
Adopting the traditional culture of Chalacta to honor her slain parents, Depa Billaba offers an ordered perspective to the wide-ranging minds of the Council.

Adi Gallia
Born into a highly placed diplomatic family stationed on Coruscant, the intuitive Adi Gallia often seems to know what people are about to say. Gallia has many contacts throughout the Coruscant political machine, making her one of the Supreme Chancellor's most valuable sources of intelligence.

Jedi robe

Gallia's second lightsaber replaces her first, which was destroyed on a mission

Protective goggles

Antiox mask

Highly developed extrasensory organs

PLO KOON
A Kel Dor from Dorin, Plo Koon must protect his sensitive eyes and nostrils from the oxygen-rich atmosphere of Coruscant with special devices.

Youthful topknot

Yaddle
Young at only 477, Jedi Master Yaddle looks up to Yoda while leading the Council with compassion and balanced patience. Yaddle silently waits in discussions before offering her single, powerful, soft-spoken comment.

DATA FILE
› The 12 High Council members reflect a mere hint of the diversity within the Jedi ranks, which include members of hundreds of species and cultures.

› Of the teeming trillions of species that populate the galaxy, very few individuals become full-fledged Jedi Knights: the ranks based on Coruscant number only about 10,000.

JEDI BLOOD
TEST KIT

Qui-Gon Jinn
JEDI MASTER

MASTER QUI-GON JINN is an experienced Jedi who has proven his value to the leadership of the Jedi order in many important missions and difficult negotiations. In his maturity, however, he remains as restless as he was in his youth. When Qui-Gon encounters young Anakin Skywalker on the Outer Rim desert world of Tatooine, the Jedi is deeply struck by an unshakeable sense that the boy is part of the galaxy's destiny. In boldly championing the cause of Anakin, Qui-Gon sets in motion momentous events that will ultimately bring balance to the Force—but not without great cost.

On the desert planet of Tatooine, Qui-Gon wishes to avoid being recognized as a Jedi. Accordingly, he trades his customary Jedi robe for a rough-spun poncho such as those worn by local settlers and moisture farmers.

REPUBLIC CRUISER
Dispatched by the Supreme Chancellor of the Galactic Senate to settle the Trade Federation dispute, Qui-Gon travels on board the diplomatic vessel *Radiant VII*.

As the *Radiant VII* prepares to land within the Trade Federation flagship's hangar, navigation readouts ensure precise maneuvers.

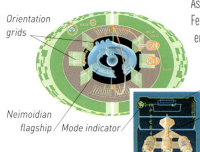

Orientation grids

Neimoidian flagship

Mode indicator

Trajectory path shows route ahead

Radiant VII

DESTINATION NAVISPHERE

Lightsaber

Following the custom of his day, Qui-Gon has built a lightsaber with a highly elaborate internal design. Multiple small power cells are stored in the scalloped handgrip and microscopic circuitry governs the nature of the energy blade. Simpler lightsaber designs, built outside the halls of the Jedi Temple on Coruscant, typically use a single large power cell inside a solid handgrip.

Qui-Gon has risen to great prominence within the Jedi order, and is well-known to the members of the High Council. Yet in spite of his outstanding service as a Jedi Knight and Master, Qui-Gon has been passed by for a seat on the Council. This is due to his bold, headstrong nature and his favoring of risk and action, which sometimes bring him into disagreement with his Jedi peers and elders.

Long hair worn back to keep vision clear

Jedi robe

Jedi tunic

Blade projection plate

Activator

Series of micro-cells

Charging port

QUI-GON JINN'S LIGHTSABER

Rugged travel boots

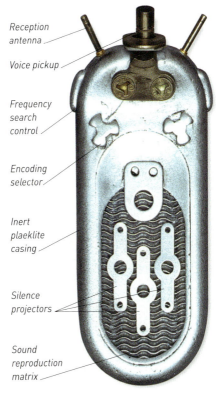

Reception antenna

Voice pickup

Frequency search control

Encoding selector

Inert plaeklite casing

Silence projectors

Sound reproduction matrix

Holoprojector

One of the utility devices that Qui-Gon carries is a small holoprojector. This can be tuned with a comlink to carry a hologram transmission for face-to-face contact, or it can be used as an independent image recorder and projector.

Qui-Gon loads his holoprojector with selected images from the technical databanks onboard the Naboo Royal Starship. He intends to use them to help obtain repair parts when the ship is grounded on Tatooine.

Tines rotate downward to plug into signal feed or to link to larger image projector

Casing ring

Sturdy construction for field use

Projection platform

Comlink

Qui-Gon's miniature comlink allows him to keep in touch with Obi-Wan Kenobi when the two operate separately. It features complex security devices to prevent unauthorized interception and is unlabeled to thwart use by non-Jedi. A silence projector lends privacy to conversations and helps Qui-Gon maintain stealth in the field.

COMLINK REVERSE VIEW

TOYDARIAN TROUBLE

Some species are naturally immune to the "Jedi mind tricks" of all but the most powerful Masters. Qui-Gon Jinn has never even heard of a Toydarian before he encounters Watto on Tatooine and the Jedi soon finds that he needs more than Force-assisted "suggestions" to persuade the hovering junk dealer to cooperate with him.

On meeting Anakin, Qui-Gon believes he has recognized the prophesied individual who will restore balance and harmony to the Force. The Jedi feels so strongly that he has recognized this individual that he is not persuaded otherwise by members of the Jedi High Council, including the influential Yoda, who sense danger in the boy.

Qui-Gon earned the rank of Master when he trained his first Padawan apprentice to Knighthood, although his second apprentice failed to become a Knight. Obi-Wan is Qui-Gon's third Padawan and a worthy student of his wisdom and skill.

On Tatooine, Qui-Gon battles a Sith warrior wielding a deadly lightsaber. Since lightsabers are seldom handled by non-Jedi, the order primarily uses them as defense against blaster bolts rather than other lightsabers. However, lightsaber dueling is taught as part of classical Jedi training.

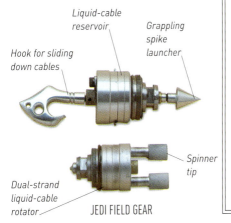

Liquid-cable reservoir

Grappling spike launcher

Hook for sliding down cables

Dual-strand liquid-cable rotator

Spinner tip

JEDI FIELD GEAR

DATA FILE

> The Jedi workshops on Coruscant supply exquisite materials and tools for initiates constructing their own lightsabers. The initiates' ability to do this successfully proves their developed sensitivity to the Force.

> Greed and political scheming are weakening the Galactic Republic that Qui-Gon serves. In an attempt to restore lasting peace and security to the galaxy, Qui-Gon is motivated to take a more active role than that traditionally taken by the Jedi.

Obi-Wan Kenobi
JEDI KNIGHT

Short hair of a Padawan apprentice

Apprentice's long braid

Tunic

Hooded robe

OBI-WAN KENOBI has followed a responsible path on his journey toward Jedi knighthood as the Padawan apprentice to Jedi Master Qui-Gon Jinn. Strongly influenced by other leading Jedi as well as by Qui-Gon, Obi-Wan is more brooding and cautious than his teacher. He is careful to weigh the consequences of his actions and is reluctant to entangle himself unnecessarily in transgressions against the will of the Jedi High Council. A serious, quiet man possessed of a dry sense of humor, Obi-Wan strives to be worthy of his order and feels honored to be Qui-Gon's student, although he worries about his Master's tendency to take risks in defiance of the Council. Nevertheless, Obi-Wan follows Qui-Gon Jinn's example and develops an independent spirit of his own.

UTILITY BELT

Belt fastener

Fastener band

Utility belt

Traditional leather

Food and tool pouches

Jedi Gear

The basic Jedi clothing of belted tunic, travel boots, and robe speaks of the simplicity vested in Jedi philosophy and carries overtones of their mission as travelers. Individual Jedi keep utility belt field gear to a minimum. As initiates are taught in the great Temple, Jedi reputations are based on their spirits and not on material trappings.

BREATHER POUCH

UTILITY POUCHES
On field missions, Jedi carry a basic kit consisting of food capsules, medical supplies, multitools, and other essential devices.

FOOD AND ENERGY CAPSULES

Rugged travel boots

A99 Aquata Breather

In this era, Jedi Knights usually carry various high-tech devices concealed in their robes or in belt pouches. On their mission to Naboo, Obi-Wan and Qui-Gon Jinn carry A99 Aquata breathers, knowing that much of the planet's surface is water. Breathers allow the Jedi to survive underwater for up to two hours. In other times, Jedi have avoided such technological devices in order to minimize their dependence on anything but their own resourcefulness.

Regulator

Hinges for storage

Mouthpiece

Compressed air tanks

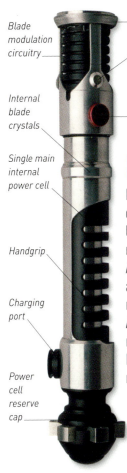

Blade modulation circuitry

Blade emitter

Blade length and intensity control

Internal blade crystals

Activator

Single main internal power cell

Handgrip

Charging port

Power cell reserve cap

Faced with the mechanized minions of the Trade Federation droid army, Obi-Wan knows that he need not exercise the combat restraint he would use with living beings. He puts his fight training to good use, yet maintains cool concentration.

Lightsaber

Lightsabers follow a common design. Optional elements, like blade power and length modulators, are small and unobtrusive. Accordingly, Jedi lightsabers appear similar at first glance. A closer inspection, however, reveals that lightsabers rarely look exactly alike. All are hand-built by the initiates themselves, making design details a matter of individual choice. Most Padawan apprentices build their lightsabers to resemble those of their teachers as a mark of respect.

Encoder

Voice pickup

Silencer

OBI-WAN KENOBI'S COMLINK

Centered awareness

Battle stance

Hyperdrive diagnostic monitor

Warning mark indicates energy leak

Damaged priming pylons

Blue lightsaber blade

Obi-Wan Kenobi views Anakin Skywalker as an unnecessary risk, both as a travel companion and as a potential Jedi. But at Qui-Gon Jinn's request, Obi-Wan accepts Anakin as his apprentice, beginning a long and fateful relationship.

Hyperdrive

When the hyperdrive generator of the Naboo Royal Starship is damaged, Obi-Wan stays on board to look after the drive core while Qui-Gon seeks a replacement generator. Constantly monitoring the damaged component, Obi-Wan readies the core for repairs.

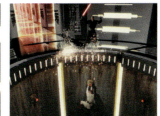

Obi-Wan is an exceptional lightsaber duelist and a formidable opponent for Darth Maul. The Sith Lord fights with inhuman intensity, fueled by the hateful energy of the dark side of the Force. In the heat of mortal combat and on the brink of death, Obi-Wan faces the temptation to draw on the same terrible strength in order to defeat his enemy.

DATA FILE

› Jedi robes are virtually indistinguishable from the simple robes worn by many species throughout the galaxy. This signifies the Jedi pledge to the service and protection of even the most humble galactic citizen.

› Obi-Wan remains loyal to Qui-Gon even when this puts him at odds with the Jedi High Council.

Data goggles allow pilot to see constant holographic data readouts

Comlink

Vessel command officer's miter

Skin mottled from self-indulgence

The Invasion Force

WHEN THE BLOCKADE fails to intimidate the Naboo Queen into submission, the Trade Federation prepares for the next step: invasion. The Sith Lord Darth Sidious persuades Neimoidian Viceroy Nute Gunray to order the deployment of an immense secret army hidden in the cargo hangars of converted trade freighters. The Naboo little suspect the magnitude of this force, and the Neimoidian leader commits the outrage in confidence that the weak politicians of the Galactic Senate will not object. In support of his evil plans, the viceroy is aided by the cowardly captain of the war fleet command vessel, Daultay Dofine, as well as droid soldiers and powerful war craft.

Daultay Dofine reports to Neimoidian Viceroy Nute Gunray.

Daultay Dofine

Captain of the Trade Federation's flagship vessel, Daultay Dofine has climbed the ladder of rank through a combination of high birth, back-stabbing, and groveling behavior toward his superiors. Nevertheless, Dofine finds the bold plans of the Sith Lord Darth Sidious too dangerous for his tastes. However, he soon learns that his tastes are entirely irrelevant.

Officer's drape

A fleet of specially built C-9979 landing craft land the Trade Federation invasion force on Naboo. These are built to hold heavy armor and legions of troops in their bodies and repulsorlift wings. Groups of three are deployed in a pattern that cuts off all the Naboo cities from each other.

MTTs are dispatched to strategic positions, where they thunder along programmed routes.

Droid deployment hatch

Heavy armor plating

Repulsorlift exhaust system

DATA FILE

❯ Wargame exercises and action against bandits threatening trade routes tested all aspects of the Trade Federation army, ensuring that the force is completely invincible... or so it seems.

❯ The wealthy, arrogant Neimoidians tend to avoid any kind of labor, preferring to use droids instead.

Although Trade Federation war craft have only been used in exercises and skirmishes before their deployment on Naboo, their cheap paint is already badly chipped. This attests to the Neimoidians' dedication to cheapness even in this profitable and long-awaited enterprise.

Protocol droid TC-14 ignores the foul play brewing against the Jedi ambassadors for the Supreme Chancellor. When the Jedi visitors are hit with poison gas, TC-14 simply wants to get out of the way, apologizing even to the battle droids outside the meeting room.

Underestimating the number of blaster turrets bristling from the Trade Federation war freighters, Naboo pilot Ric Olié takes a near-collision course in his effort to escape the deadly line of fire.

TC-14

Serving Viceroy Nute Gunray and his lieutenant Rune Haako of the Trade Federation, TC-14 acts as servant and translator during trade negotiations with foreign cultures. TC-14 is often employed to distract official guests while legal manipulation is carried out behind their backs.

Frequent memory erasures ensure docility

Neutral humanoid form

Restraining bolt mount

Multi-system connection wires

Subservient posture

Polished silver finish

Reinforced knee joint

Shinplate

Foot shell

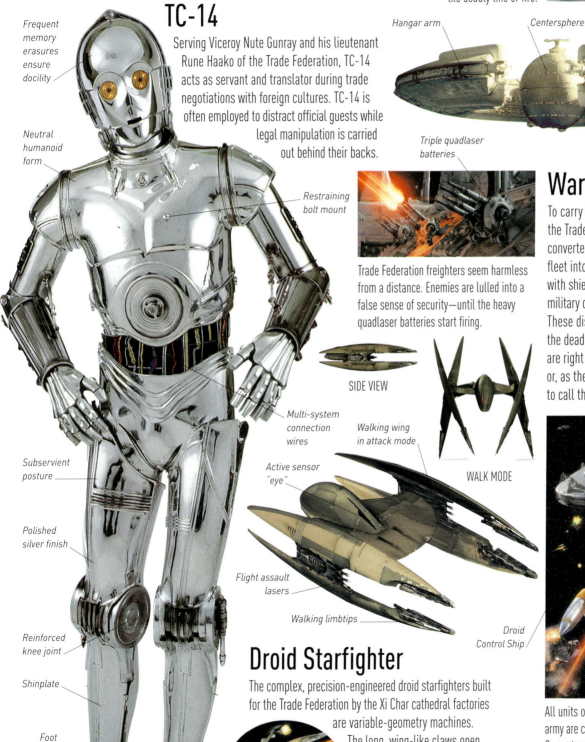

Hangar arm *Centersphere* *War forces carried in interior*

Triple quadlaser batteries

Armor-plated hull

Trade Federation freighters seem harmless from a distance. Enemies are lulled into a false sense of security—until the heavy quadlaser batteries start firing.

War Freighter

To carry the forces of its army, the Trade Federation has secretly converted its commercial freighter fleet into battleships, replete with shields, blaster turrets, and military communication arrays. These disguised war freighters hide the deadly battle machines until they are right on top of their enemies— or, as the Trade Federation prefers to call them, "future customers."

SIDE VIEW

WALK MODE

Walking wing in attack mode

Active sensor "eye"

Flight assault lasers

Walking limbtips

Droid Starfighter

The complex, precision-engineered droid starfighters built for the Trade Federation by the Xi Char cathedral factories are variable-geometry machines. The long, wing-like claws open to reveal deadly laser cannons. On the ground, these "wings" become movable legs as the fighter shifts to walk mode for surface patrol.

Droid Control Ship

All units of the Trade Federation droid army are controlled by the Central Control Computer onboard a modified war freighter. Without the control signal, droids shut down, making the Droid Control Ship a key target whose destruction could wipe out the entire invasion force.

Battle Droids

THE GALACTIC REPUBLIC has survived disagreements, standoffs, and even rebellion among its many member worlds, relying on the Jedi Knights to quell conflicts. In this enlightened age, few standing armies are maintained that serve anything other than ceremonial purposes, since an army could be regarded as an open threat to galactic peace. Nevertheless, as the bureaucracy of the Republic Senate indulges in endless debates and procedural bickering, the use of force has become a real threat. The wealthy Trade Federation has quietly gone far beyond any other group in assembling a massive army composed of ghostly, emotionless droid soldiers that are ready to do their masters' bidding without a touch of emotion or mercy. Their deployment upon the peaceful people of Naboo heralds the end of an age of peace and security in the galaxy.

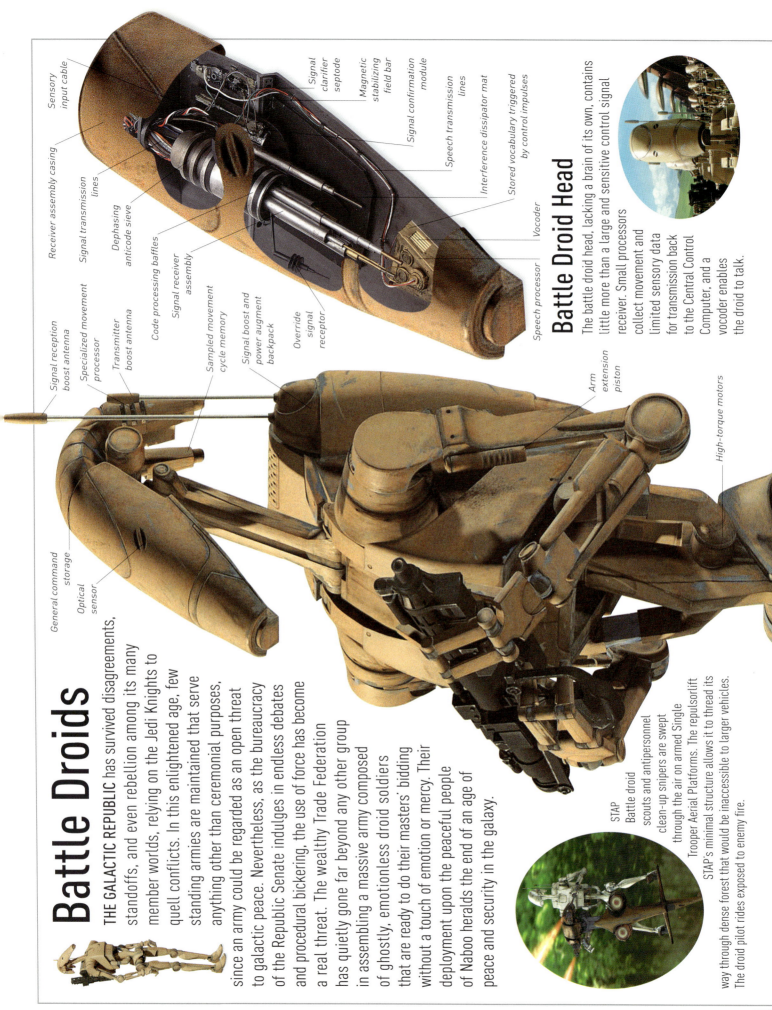

Sensory input cable

Receiver assembly casing

Signal transmission lines

Dephasing anticode sieve

Signal clarifier septode

Magnetic stabilizing field bar

Signal confirmation module

Speech transmission lines

Interference dissipator mat

Stored vocabulary triggered by control impulses

Vocoder

Speech processor

Code processing baffles

Signal receiver assembly

Sampled movement cycle memory

Signal boost and power augment backpack

Override signal receptor

Signal reception boost antenna

Specialized movement processor

Transmitter boost antenna

General command storage

Optical sensor

Arm extension piston

High-torque motors

Battle Droid Head

The battle droid head, lacking a brain of its own, contains little more than a large and sensitive control signal receiver. Small processors collect movement and limited sensory data for transmission back to the Central Control Computer, and a vocoder enables the droid to talk.

STAP

Battle droid scouts and antipersonnel clean-up snipers are swept through the air on an armed Single Trooper Aerial Platforms. The repulsorlift STAP's minimal structure allows it to thread its way through dense forest that would be inaccessible to larger vehicles. The droid pilot rides exposed to enemy fire.

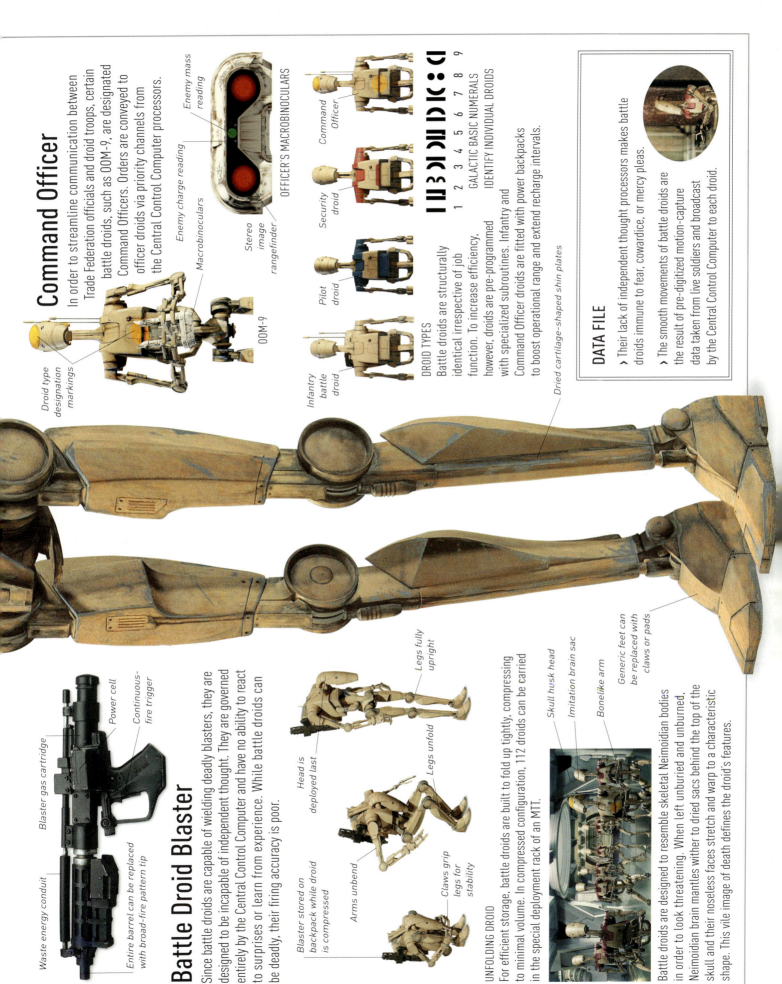

Command Officer

In order to streamline communication between Trade Federation officials and droid troops, certain battle droids, such as OOM-9, are designated Command Officers. Orders are conveyed to officer droids via priority channels from the Central Control Computer processors.

Enemy mass reading

Enemy charge reading

Macrobinoculars

Stereo image rangefinder

OFFICER'S MACROBINOCULARS

OOM-9

Droid type designation markings

DROID TYPES

Battle droids are structurally identical irrespective of job function. To increase efficiency, however, droids are pre-programmed with specialized subroutines. Infantry and Command Officer droids are fitted with power backpacks to boost operational range and extend recharge intervals.

Command Officer

Security droid

Pilot droid

Infantry battle droid

ⵘ ⵗ ⵗ ⵗ ⵗ ⵗ ⵗ ⵗ ⵗ ⵗ
1 2 3 4 5 6 7 8 9
GALACTIC BASIC NUMERALS IDENTIFY INDIVIDUAL DROIDS

Dried cartilage-shaped shin plates

DATA FILE

➤ Their lack of independent thought processors makes battle droids immune to fear, cowardice, or mercy pleas.

➤ The smooth movements of battle droids are the result of pre-digitized motion-capture data taken from live soldiers and broadcast by the Central Control Computer to each droid.

Generic feet can be replaced with claws or pads

Skull husk head

Imitation brain sac

Bonelike arm

Battle Droid Blaster

Since battle droids are capable of wielding deadly blasters, they are designed to be incapable of independent thought. They are governed entirely by the Central Control Computer and have no ability to react to surprises or learn from experience. While battle droids can be deadly, their firing accuracy is poor.

Waste energy conduit

Blaster gas cartridge

Power cell

Continuous-fire trigger

Entire barrel can be replaced with broad-fire pattern tip

Legs fully upright

Head is deployed last

Legs unfold

Blaster stored on backpack while droid is compressed

Arms unbend

Claws grip legs for stability

UNFOLDING DROID

For efficient storage, battle droids are built to fold up tightly, compressing to minimal volume. In compressed configuration, 112 droids can be carried in the special deployment rack of an MTT.

Battle droids are designed to resemble skeletal Neimoidian bodies in order to look threatening. When left unburied and unburned, Neimoidian brain mantles wither to dried sacs behind the top of the skull and their noseless faces stretch and warp to a characteristic shape. This vile image of death defines the droid's features.

Droidekas

TO MAKE UP for the weaknesses of battle droids, a special contract was awarded for the creation of an altogether different combat droid that would be a much more serious weapon. The design was created by a species of chitinous Colicoids in their own image on a planet far from the Republic's core. Colicoids are known for their completely unfeeling and murderous ways, and Colla IV has been embroiled for many years in diplomatic disputes related to the death and consumption of visitors to the system. The droideka was exactly what concerned Trade Federation officers wanted: a formidable, heavy-duty killing machine to back up the battle droids in the face of determined opposition.

Using a combination of momentum and repulsor effects, droidekas unfurl in a matter of seconds from wheel form into standing position, ready to attack. The dramatic transformation recalls the attack pattern of a deadly adult Colicoid, and can take unwary opponents by surprise—as the droids' manufacturers intended.

FRONT VIEW

Head-on to an attacker, a droideka presents blazing guns and a fearsome image as well as a minimal target silhouette for opponents who survive long enough to return fire.

Triad active sensor antennae

Case-hardened bronzium armor shell

Reactor cooling vanes

BACK VIEW

Desperate enemies attempting to attack a droideka from behind find that its armor is extremely effective, and its moving legs and gun arms are hard to hit.

Rear leg

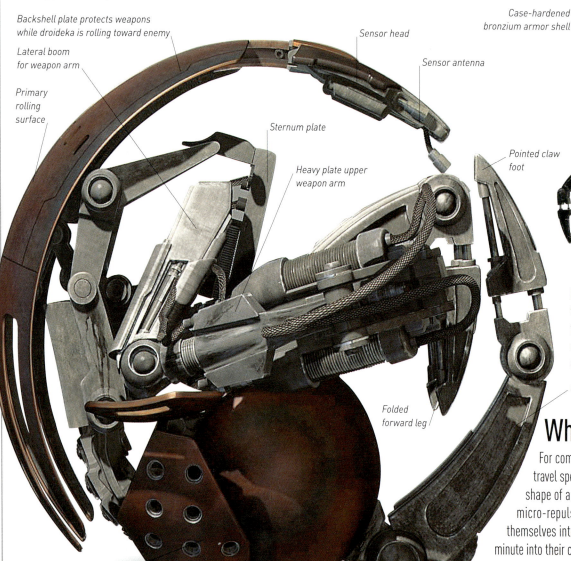

Backshell plate protects weapons while droideka is rolling toward enemy

Lateral boom for weapon arm

Primary rolling surface

Sensor head

Sensor antenna

Sternum plate

Heavy plate upper weapon arm

Pointed claw foot

Folded forward leg

Deflector shield projector flaps

Wheel Form

For compact storage and optimum travel speed, droidekas retract into the shape of a wheel. Using pulsed internal micro-repulsors in sequence, they roll themselves into battle, opening at the last minute into their combat form. In transit, the wheel configuration presents a smaller and faster target to enemy gunfire.

Qui-Gon Jinn and Obi-Wan Kenobi evade or cut down battle droids with relative ease. But when droidekas attack, the Jedi cannot hold them off indefinitely and Qui-Gon knows they must escape.

Covered with heavy alloy or armor plate, droidekas are fearsome specters that cut down soldiers by the dozen with ease. They also carry their own deflector shield generators that can completely repel pistol fire and substantially weaken high-energy rifle or artillery bolts. This makes them nearly invincible in combat.

Sensor head

Non-visual composite radiation sensor antennae

Primary sensor antenna

Blaster power converter

Arm extensor strut

Twin high-energy blaster

Collimating tip concentrates blaster bolt energy

Blaster energizer

Blaster power cable

Hip joint

Backshell plate

Pneumatic pressure conduit

Pneumatic limb charger

Sternum plate

Power cable

Spinal power cell series

Blaster heat dissipator cowl

Deflector shield projector plate

Mini-reactor bulb

Case-hardened bronzium armor bulb protects reactor

Repulsor lifts droid

Legs guide droid

Shield plates open in combat stance

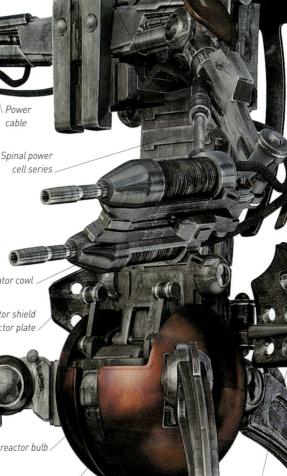

Combat Stance

When a droideka is ready to begin an assault, it quickly unfolds and stands up on three legs. Its pneumatic arms flex open and its eerie head rises with its enemy-finding sensors ablaze. Made only for combat and specialized for the single purpose of destruction, the droideka has no need of hands. Instead, powerful twin blasters are built onto its arms.

Droidekas generate shields using on-board mini-reactors contained in their armored bases. These reactors also power the droids' volt-guzzling movement systems and high-energy blasters.

DATA FILE

› Like battle droids, droidekas lack independent logic processors and are run by signals from the Central Control Computer. The Colicoids dislike this system and have built custom droidekas equipped with computer brains.

› Droidekas are commonly known as destroyer droids in many parts of the galaxy.

Foot claw designed for hard surfaces

Queen Amidala

AMIDALA rules as Queen of the Naboo people at the age of only 14. She was raised by humble parents in a small mountain village, where her exceptional abilities were recognized early in life. Given the best training and pushed to develop her capabilities, she became Princess of Theed, the Naboo capital city, at the age of 12. Amidala was elected Queen upon the abdication of the previous sovereign, Veruna, who had become embroiled in outworld politics after a rule of 13 years. The Naboo trusted that Amidala would hold their interests close to her heart—but had no idea of the crisis looming ahead.

Jewel of Zenda

Gold faceframes

Hair combed over a padded form

Wide shoulders make Amidala seem larger

Hand-stitched gold embroidery

White thumbnail polish is the only tradition Amidala retains from her native village

Foreknot

Beaded emblems over 240 years old, taken from an earlier queen's gown

Suspensas

Large oversleeves

Painted thumbnail

Black Cyrene silk fabric

Feet hidden for stateliness

FOREIGN RESIDENCE GOWN

On Coruscant, Amidala wears a dark gown befitting the gravity of her situation. This subdued foreign residence gown acknowledges Amidala's separation from Naboo and the peril her people face.

Throne-Room Gown

Amidala draws upon Naboo's deeply traditional modes of royal dress and makeup to express the commitment she has to her role. Her extremely formal appearance in the palace throne room helps her project an unwaveringly professional image and warns others not to dismiss her abilities.

Amidala sits in state in Theed Palace, hearing cases and reports from the Advisory Council. With her clear perception, she inspires confidence even in seasoned and hard-edged men like Captain Panaka.

Shed potolli fur cuffs

Illuminated sein jewel

Wide gown flare hides feet

Antique tiara

Mauve chersilk hair veil

Drapa bindings

Full cerlin sleeves

Multilayered gown

AMIDALA'S TRAVELING GOWN

When Queen Amidala travels aboard the Naboo Royal Starship, she holds court in a spacious throne room. Amidala uses a holoprojector to communicate with Governor Sio Bibble back on Naboo.

GOLD BEADS

The Queen's gowns are set off with many fine details, such as beads and suspensa ornaments. Many of these come from the palace treasure rooms.

Amidala's stylized white makeup draws upon Naboo's ancient royal customs. The red "scar of remembrance" marks Naboo's time of suffering, before the Great Time of Peace.

NABOO VICTORY PARADE

Scar of remembrance divides lip

Stylized beauty marks display symmetry

Golden hairbands

Escoffiate headpiece

Royal Sovereign of Naboo medal

Royal diadem

Minimal jewelry for simplicity

Aurate fan in ancient Naboo royal fashion, signifying continuity

Jeweled finials

Senate Gown

When Amidala pleads for her people before the Galactic Senate, she appears in an extraordinary gown and hairstyle that express the majesty of the free people of Naboo. The regal attire also hides Amidala's feelings and helps her stay courageous and aloof.

Suspensas made of delicate orichalc finework

Grand finial hairtip ornaments balance escoffiate headpiece

Petaled cape

Golden, triple-braided soutache

Plain white gown expresses the pure happiness of new found peace

Embossed rosette

Parade Gown

After the victory over the Trade Federation, Amidala appears in a parade gown markedly different from her robes of office. The silken petals of the dress resemble huge, lovely flowers found near Amidala's home village. These flowers bloom only once every 88 years, heralding a time of special celebration.

DATA FILE

‣ Naboo's monarchy is not hereditary: rulers are elected by their people on merit. Queen Amidala is not the youngest sovereign ever to rule.

‣ Amidala can step down from the throne whenever she chooses.

Naboo Pilots

LIKE THEIR COMRADES the Security Guard and the Palace Guard, the Space Fighter Corps is a unit of the Royal Naboo Security Forces. Its pilots are a devil-may-care lot from diverse backgrounds who fly the custom-built Naboo N-1 Starfighters with pride. Their usual missions are routine patrols, escort duties, or parade flights. Lack of combat on peaceful Naboo forces the pilots to gain experience off-planet in Republic pirate fighter groups or on the rare patrol missions that encounter troublemakers. By no means the most dangerous bunch of space pilots in the galaxy, the Space Fighter Corps are nonetheless ready for action—even in the face of the Trade Federation's overwhelming challenge.

Flying goggles

Anti-glare brim

Built-in communicator system

Flying jacket

Space Fighter Corps overcoat

Pilot safety harness attaches to ship's seat

Bright colors typical of Naboo style

Flying gloves

Naboo pilot-issue boots

N-1 Starfighter

Partly finished in gleaming chromium to indicate royal status, N-1 Starfighters sport radial engines of Nubian make in a J-configuration spaceframe. Assisted by an astromech droid, starfighters are fast and agile, but prone to uncontrollable spins when the engines suffer damage.

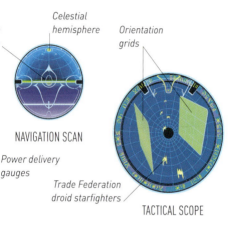

Power diversion display

Reference horizon

Celestial hemisphere

Orientation grids

Power delivery gauges

Trade Federation droid starfighters

SYSTEMS MONITOR

NAVIGATION SCAN

TACTICAL SCOPE

N-1 STARFIGHTER READOUTS
Starfighter pilots constantly monitor navigation and systems information from readout panels arrayed in the cockpit.

Welded joints of armor shell

Automatic distress beacon

FLYING HELMET

Ric Olié

The top pilot in the Space Fighter Corps is Ric Olié, a veteran flier who answers directly to Captain Panaka. Perfectly capable of flying any craft on Naboo, it is Ric Olié's honor to captain the Queen's Royal Starship. The run through the Trade Federation blockade taxes Olié's flying abilities to the limit, and even he doubts whether they can get through alive.

DATA FILE

› Naboo pilots must gain experience flying utility craft before they are permitted to take the controls of a coveted N-1 Starfighter.

› Only a few lucky pilots have ever flown royal escort duty all the way to Coruscant, most never having left Naboo's sector.

R2-D2
NABOO DROID

A UTILITY DROID with a mind of his own, there is more to R2-D2 than his ordinary appearance would suggest. Just one of several droids assigned to the Naboo Royal Starship, R2-D2 replaces blown fuses, installs new wiring, polishes floors, and does whatever else is necessary to maintain the gleaming vessel in perfect working condition. For a utility droid, R2-D2 is equipped with remarkable tenacity and drive to accomplish his missions. Such dedication would ordinarily go unnoticed, but when a crisis envelops the Royal Starship, R2-D2 becomes a hero.

DROID HOLD
In a small chamber on the lowest deck of the Naboo Royal Starship, R2-D2 recharges between work projects and waits with other astromech droids for assignments. A repulsorlift tube at one end of the hold conveys the droids to the outside of the ship for work on the hull during flight.

Astromech droid repair-monitor image

R2-D2 at work on the hull

Damaged deflector shield generator

IN-FLIGHT REPAIRS
Astromech droids commonly carry out a wide variety of mechanical repair and information retrieval tasks. R2-D2 does not stand out from the crowd until he singlehandedly completes repairs to the Naboo Royal Starship's shield generator.

CO-PILOT
Standard astromech droids are used in many space fighters as onboard flight support. R2-D2 accompanies Anakin Skywalker into battle in the droid socket of a Naboo N-1 Starfighter.

Secondary holographic projector

Primary photoreceptor and radar eye

Luminescent diagnostic display

Hydraulic arm shaft

Heat exhaust

Hydraulic extension arm

Optional oxidizer intake

Pneumatic cleaner

Sonic welder

Thrust nozzle

Deployment brace

REPAIR ARM
This extendible arm can clean, cut, or seal electronic components.

ROCKET THRUSTER
Accessory rocket thrusters give R2 units the ability to propel themselves through air or space.

Control impulse and power net linkage

Inference pulse stabilizers

Sand-proof joints

Extendible third leg

Swivel-mounted tread

All-terrain main drive tread

Powerbus cables

DATA FILE

› R2-D2 is owned by the Royal House of Naboo. He was assigned to the Queen's ship because of his outstanding performance record.

› R2's head can telescope up so that he can see out of the tight neck of a Naboo Starfighter droid socket.

Jar Jar Binks

AN AMPHIBIOUS GUNGAN native to Naboo, Jar Jar is a luckless exile from his home city, Otoh Gunga. He now lives in the swamps, where he survives on his own, eating raw shellfish and other such swamp fare. His long muscular tongue helps him to scoop mollusks out of their shells and tasty gumbols out of their tree burrows. During the invasion of Naboo, Qui-Gon Jinn runs into and rescues Jar Jar. The simple Gungan's sense of honor binds him to Qui-Gon for life, even though the Jedi would much rather do without him at first.

At first, Obi-Wan Kenobi dismisses Jar Jar as an inconvenient life form to have around. However, the Gungan quickly proves useful by telling the Jedi of an underwater city where they can escape from the ground forces of the Trade Federation.

Gungan Survivor

Like all Gungans, Jar Jar's skeleton is made of cartilage, making him flexible and rubbery. Even his skull and jaws are elastic, giving the simple Gungan a wide range of facial expressions. Jar Jar's character, like his body, is resilient and able to bend to changes of fortune without letting his spirit break. Whether alone, in the company of Jedi, or even among royalty, Jar Jar blunders through life with light-hearted good humor in spite of his occasional panic attacks.

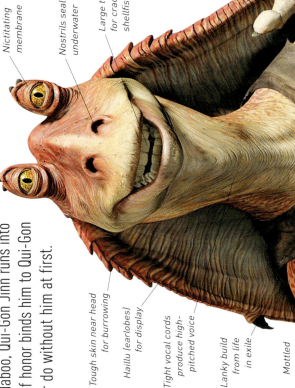

Jar Jar is reticent about the reason for his exile from Otoh Gunga, glossing over the fact that he accidentally flooded most of Boss Nass's mansion and several adjoining bubbles while working as a waiter at a high-class party. As this was not Jar Jar's first serious accident, or even his first serious flooding accident, Boss Nass was furious, and Jar Jar was exiled from his own city under pain of death.

Jar Jar is well known to the city patrol of Otoh Gunga, which has extricated him from all kinds of trouble in the past—from petty squabbles over food theft to the commotion Jar Jar caused when he inadvertently opened half of the Otoh Gunga Zoo bubbles. They know Boss Nass will not be pleased to see the infamous Gungan in his chambers again.

Partially retractable eyestalk

Nictitating membrane

Nostrils seal underwater

Large teeth for cracking shellfish

Tough skin near head for burrowing

Haillu (earlobes) for display

Tight vocal cords produce high-pitched voice

Lanky build from life in exile

Mottled skin for camouflage

Fashion statement

Mollusk and gumbol breakfast

GUNGAN HANDCUFFS

Four-fingered hand

Cartilaginous skeleton is stiff but not brittle

When Qui-Gon Jinn goes to Mos Espa in search of hyperdrive parts, Jar Jar accompanies him. Qui-Gon knows that this odd Gungan will help him blend into the diverse population of strange life forms inhabiting the city. Meanwhile, Jar Jar worries about exposing his amphibian skin to the heat and suns.

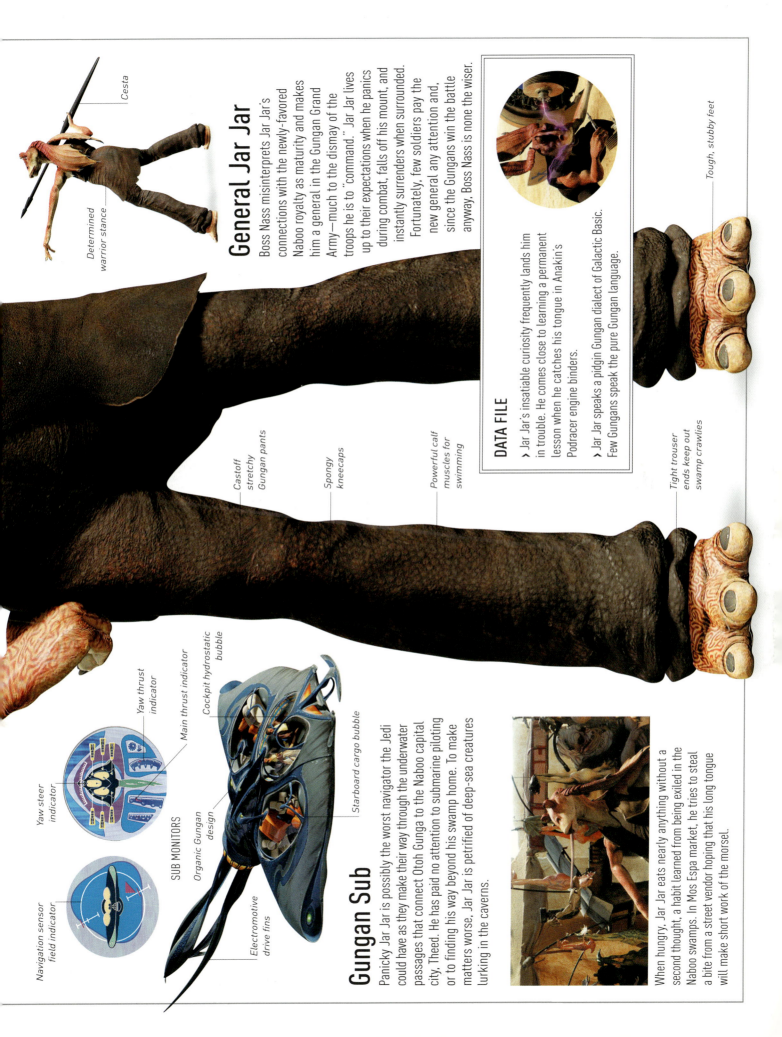

Cesta

Determined
warrior stance

General Jar Jar

Boss Nass misinterprets Jar Jar's connections with the newly-favored Naboo royalty as maturity and makes him a general in the Gungan Grand Army—much to the dismay of the troops he is to "command." Jar Jar lives up to their expectations when he panics during combat, falls off his mount, and instantly surrenders when surrounded. Fortunately, few soldiers pay the new general any attention and, since the Gungans win the battle anyway, Boss Nass is none the wiser.

DATA FILE

➤ Jar Jar's insatiable curiosity frequently lands him in trouble. He comes close to learning a permanent lesson when he catches his tongue in Anakin's Podracer engine binders.

➤ Jar Jar speaks a pidgin Gungan dialect of Galactic Basic. Few Gungans speak the pure Gungan language.

Castoff
stretchy
Gungan pants

Spongy
kneecaps

Powerful calf
muscles for
swimming

Tight trouser
ends keep out
swamp crawlies

Tough, stubby feet

Gungan Sub

Panicky Jar Jar is possibly the worst navigator the Jedi could have as they make their way through the underwater passages that connect Otoh Gunga to the Naboo capital city, Theed. He has paid no attention to submarine piloting or to finding his way beyond his swamp home. To make matters worse, Jar Jar is petrified of deep-sea creatures lurking in the caverns.

Navigation sensor
field indicator

Yaw steer
indicator

Yaw thrust
indicator

Main thrust indicator

Cockpit hydrostatic
bubble

Starboard cargo bubble

SUB MONITORS

Organic Gungan
design

Electromotive
drive fins

When hungry, Jar Jar eats nearly anything without a second thought, a habit learned from being exiled in the Naboo swamps. In Mos Espa market, he tries to steal a bite from a street vendor hoping that his long tongue will make short work of the morsel.

Darth Maul

FUELED BY THE AGGRESSIVE energies of the dark side, the Sith order began almost two millennia ago with a renegade Jedi who sought to use the Force to gain control. Both strengthened and twisted by the dark side, the Sith fought against each other to gain power and domination until only one remained: Darth Bane. To prevent internecine strife, Bane remade the Sith as an order that would endure in only two individuals at a time. Biding their time, the Sith lay in wait for the right moment to overturn the Jedi and seize control of the galaxy. The present Sith Master, Darth Sidious is the diabolically brilliant mind behind the training of one of the most dangerous Sith apprentices in history: the deadly Darth Maul.

Darth Sidious uses a clear and powerful hologram transmission to communicate with his Neimoidian minions and his apprentice field agent, Darth Maul. Fiercely demanding of high standards, Sidious has been known to dismiss individuals simply for communicating with too weak a signal.

Transmission antenna

Scan-absorbing stealth shell

Magnetic imaging device

External weapons mount

Thermal imager

Levitator

Primary photoreceptor

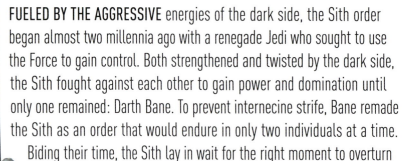

Electrobinoculars

On Tatooine, Maul uses electrobinoculars to search for the Jedi. These electrobinoculars are equipped with radiation sensors for night vision and powerful light-gathering components for long-distance scanning.

Multi-scan controls

Light-gathering lens

Power cells

Memory stores 360° horizon view

Filters screen out atmospheric interference

Nav-grid can be projected onto landscape

Range to target

Alarm signals energy sources or visual targets

Mode indicator

Magnification

ELECTROBINOCULAR VIEWSCREEN
Tied to global mapping scanners in his starship, Maul's electrobinocular viewscreen displays the precise location of targets and indicates life signals or power frequencies. Specific shapes, colors, or energy types can be set as targets, and even invisible defensive fields can be detected.

Probe Droid

Darth Maul uses elaborate technology in his work as the Sith apprentice of Darth Sidious. One of his most useful tools is the "dark eye" probe droid, a hovering reconnaissance device that can be programmed to seek out individuals or information.

"DARK EYE" DEVICES
Probe droids locate their quarry using multispectral imaging and many kinds of scanning. The probes silently monitor conversations and eavesdrop on electronic transmissions, and can be fitted with a number of small, deadly weapons.

Scanning lens attachment

Ball detonator

Darth Maul's speeder is powered by a strong repulsorlift engine for rapid acceleration and sharp cornering. The open-cockpit design allows Maul to leap directly from the speeder into battle.

Acceleration handgrips

Braking pedals

Steering bar

Open cockpit design offers optimum visibility

Repulsorlift

Maul prides himself on his abilities as a tracker, and relishes the challenge of difficult assignments given to him by his Sith master.

SITH SPEEDER
The speeder carries no weapons, since Maul prefers the direct assault of blade weapons or the treachery of bombs to the use of blasters.

Sith Apprentice

Darth Maul is one of the most highly trained Sith in the history of the order. Focusing on physical and tactical abilities, Maul serves his master obediently, believing that his own time for strategic wisdom and eventual domination will come. His face is tattooed with symbols giving evidence of his complete dedication to discipline in the dark side.

Vestigial horns

Hairless skull

Face tattoos

Gleaming yellow eyes

Dark robe

Blade projection plate

Activator

Control lock

Blade modulation control

Control lock

Gauntlets

Maul's weapon is two joined lightsabers

Ribbed handgrip

Blade modulation circuitry

Double-bladed lightsaber

Beam emitter

Field cloak cut to allow fighting movement

Lightsaber blade is red due to nature of internal crystals

Heavy-action boots

With his double-bladed lightsaber, Maul is equal to two Jedi who are unprepared for his powers. Since the Sith disappeared almost 1,000 years ago, Jedi are not used to facing opponents armed with lightsabers.

Transmission and reception antenna

Function controls

WRIST LINK

Maul's programmable wrist link allows him to remotely direct "dark eye" probe droids, arm traps, detonate bombs, and conduct other treacherous activities. It also receives signals from surveillance devices.

Maul's Lightsaber

Pushing his physical and Force-assisted abilities to the utmost, Darth Maul built and uses a double-bladed lightsaber as his primary weapon. Traditionally used only as a training device, the double-ended saber can be much more dangerous to its wielder than an enemy. In the hands of Darth Maul, however, it becomes a whirling vortex of lethal energy.

DATA FILE

› Maul's lightsaber contains two sets of internal components; one can act as backup to the other.

› Darth Maul's Sith Infiltrator spaceship is equipped with a rare cloaking device, allowing him to travel invisibly.

Anakin Skywalker

TATOOINE SLAVE

ALTHOUGH HE LOOKS like any other nine-year-old boy living on the Outer Rim planet of Tatooine, Anakin Skywalker is far from ordinary. A slave to the junk dealer Watto, Anakin lives with his mother in the spaceport city of Mos Espa. He has a natural ability with mechanical devices, quickly understanding how they work. In his spare time, Anakin repairs and builds machines, including Podracer engines and a working droid. Qui-Gon Jinn notices his keen perception and unnaturally fast reflexes, and recognizes that the Force is extraordinarily strong in Anakin.

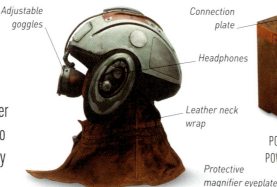

Adjustable goggles

Connection plate

Headphones

Leather neck wrap

PODRACER POWER CELL

No human has ever needed a Podracing helmet in Mos Espa, since humans ordinarily cannot ride Podracers. Anakin's extra-small helmet was made for him as a gift by Taieb, a local craftsman.

Protective magnifier eyeplate

WELDING GOGGLES

Family and Friends

Anakin's mother, Shmi, believes in Anakin and encourages him in his dreams to escape slavery on Tatooine. His best friend, Kitster, is a fellow slave who hopes someday to become a majordomo for a wealthy Mos Espa estate. Anakin's unusual talents sometimes distance him from his friends, but Kitster has always been loyal.

Necklace given to Anakin by his mother

Slave's simple haircut

Arm wraps

Anakin has his own room in the Skywalker home. Electronic and mechanical components are piled around his bed since Anakin is constantly tinkering and trying to figure things out. Working for Watto gives Anakin opportunities for picking up scrap equipment here and there.

Slave and Dreamer

Anakin has been raised by his mother to believe in himself. She has given him faith in his dreams in spite of their humble situation as slaves. Anakin looks forward to the day when he will be free to pilot starships of the mainline through the spacelanes of the galaxy. He soon finds that belief in one's dreams can have powerful results.

Among Anakin's friends is Wald, a young Rodian who speaks Huttese. Wald doubts Anakin's extraordinary abilities.

KITSTER

Tool pouch

Survival flares for use in sandstorms

Leg wraps keep out sand

Cheap, durable jumba leather

Rough work clothing

TRAVEL LUGGAGE

WUPIUPI (TATOOINE COINS)

DATA FILE

> Anakin once belonged to Gardulla the Hutt, but she lost him in a bet to Watto when Anakin was about three years old.

> As a nine-year-old boy, Anakin would never be allowed to compete in civilized Podraces, but the Outer Rim is known for its exciting free-for-all race policies.

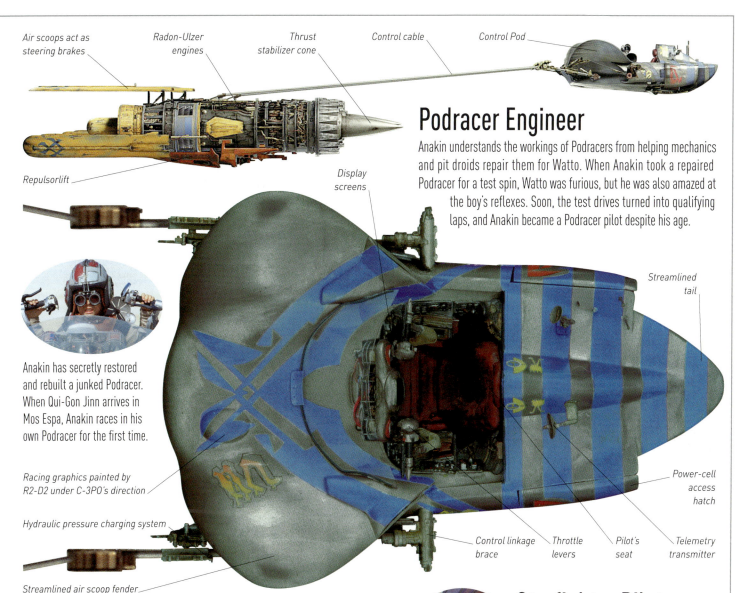

Air scoops act as steering brakes

Radon-Ulzer engines

Thrust stabilizer cone

Control cable

Control Pod

Repulsorlift

Display screens

Podracer Engineer

Anakin understands the workings of Podracers from helping mechanics and pit droids repair them for Watto. When Anakin took a repaired Podracer for a test spin, Watto was furious, but he was also amazed at the boy's reflexes. Soon, the test drives turned into qualifying laps, and Anakin became a Podracer pilot despite his age.

Streamlined tail

Anakin has secretly restored and rebuilt a junked Podracer. When Qui-Gon Jinn arrives in Mos Espa, Anakin races in his own Podracer for the first time.

Racing graphics painted by R2-D2 under C-3PO's direction

Hydraulic pressure charging system

Power-cell access hatch

Control linkage brace

Throttle levers

Pilot's seat

Telemetry transmitter

Streamlined air scoop fender

Acceleration rate indicator

Schematic view of engine mid-systems

Pressure management mode indicator

Interval velocity scale

Highlighted system near critical level

ANAKIN'S PODRACER DISPLAYS

Overpressure alarm

When his dreams start coming true faster than he can keep up, Anakin finds himself standing in the center of the Jedi Council Chamber on Coruscant. Yoda believes that the boy is too old, angry, and fearful to begin Jedi training. But Anakin is determined not to be underestimated.

Starfighter Pilot

One of Anakin's dreams is to become a starfighter pilot, and he practises in simulator games whenever possible. Most of Anakin's friends think his dreams are unrealistic, but a few people realize that there is something special about him. During the invasion of Naboo, Anakin hides in a starfighter cockpit half-knowing that he might try it out... just a little.

When the starfighter autopilot engages, the ship flies Anakin into the heart of the battle raging above. He must think furiously fast to figure out the controls before he is killed.

Crash-landing deep within the Trade Federation Droid Control Ship, Anakin accidentally fires his torpedoes into the pilot reactors, setting off a cataclysmic chain reaction.

Shmi Skywalker

WHEN PIRATES CAPTURED her parents during a space voyage in the Outer Rim, young Shmi Skywalker was sold into slavery and separated from her family. During a difficult childhood, Shmi was taken from one system to another by several masters of various species while serving as a house servant. When no longer a girl, Shmi was dropped from house servant status and was forced into cleaning work. Although slavery is illegal in the Republic, laws do not reach all parts of the galaxy—and while inexpensive droids can perform menial tasks as well as humans, living slaves give great status and prestige to their owners.

Simple hairstyle typical of servants

Rough-spun tunic withstands harsh Tatooine weather

Decorative belt

Mladong bracelet

WORKSTATION
When Shmi is not working at Watto's home, she is permitted to clean computer memory devices to bring in a modest income. A small area in their home where Shmi keeps her tools and equipment is devoted to this activity.

Aeromagnifier

Some of the tools at Shmi's workstation were given to Shmi in recognition of her service as a dependable servant. When Watto obtained an aeromagnifier in a large lot of used goods, he gave it to Shmi even though he could have sold it. The magnifier hovers in the right position to help her see what she is working on.

Repulsor hood

Magnifier

Illuminator rings

SHMI'S KITCHEN
In spite of their poverty, Shmi works hard to make a good home for herself and her son, Anakin. Her kitchen includes some labor-saving devices, but lacks the more costly moisture-conserving domes and fields, which help save precious—and expensive—water.

Spicy ahrisa *Lamta* *Haroun bread* *Sidi gourd*

MOS ESPA PRODUCE *Tezirett seed* *Driss pod*

Slave and Mother

Tantalized several times by the false possibility of freedom, Shmi now accepts her life and finds joy in her son Anakin, whom she loves dearly. Shmi and Anakin live together in the Slave Quarter of Mos Espa, a collection of adobe hovels piled together at the edge of town.

When the Jedi Master Qui-Gon Jinn recognizes Anakin's special qualities and offers to take him away to a greater destiny, only Shmi's selfless care for her son gives her the strength to let him go.

DATA FILE

❯ Shmi learned her technical skills under a former master, Pi-Lippa, who planned to grant Shmi her freedom. However, when Pi-Lippa died, Shmi was sold to a relative.

❯ Shmi can always sense when Anakin is nearby, even when she cannot see or hear him.

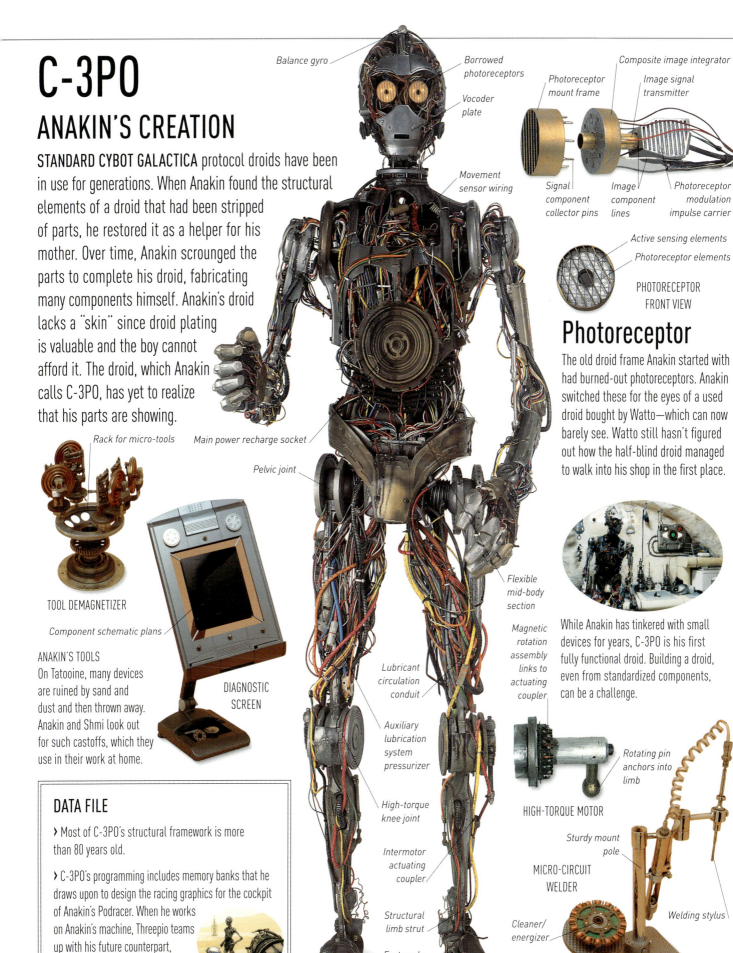

C-3PO
ANAKIN'S CREATION

STANDARD CYBOT GALACTICA protocol droids have been in use for generations. When Anakin found the structural elements of a droid that had been stripped of parts, he restored it as a helper for his mother. Over time, Anakin scrounged the parts to complete his droid, fabricating many components himself. Anakin's droid lacks a "skin" since droid plating is valuable and the boy cannot afford it. The droid, which Anakin calls C-3PO, has yet to realize that his parts are showing.

Rack for micro-tools

TOOL DEMAGNETIZER

Component schematic plans

ANAKIN'S TOOLS
On Tatooine, many devices are ruined by sand and dust and then thrown away. Anakin and Shmi look out for such castoffs, which they use in their work at home.

DIAGNOSTIC SCREEN

DATA FILE
› Most of C-3PO's structural framework is more than 80 years old.

› C-3PO's programming includes memory banks that he draws upon to design the racing graphics for the cockpit of Anakin's Podracer. When he works on Anakin's machine, Threepio teams up with his future counterpart, R2-D2, for the first time.

Balance gyro

Borrowed photoreceptors

Vocoder plate

Movement sensor wiring

Main power recharge socket

Pelvic joint

Flexible mid-body section

Lubricant circulation conduit

Auxiliary lubrication system pressurizer

High-torque knee joint

Intermotor actuating coupler

Structural limb strut

Foot angle sensor

Magnetic rotation assembly links to actuating coupler

Photoreceptor mount frame

Composite image integrator

Image signal transmitter

Signal component collector pins

Image component lines

Photoreceptor modulation impulse carrier

Active sensing elements

Photoreceptor elements

PHOTORECEPTOR FRONT VIEW

Photoreceptor
The old droid frame Anakin started with had burned-out photoreceptors. Anakin switched these for the eyes of a used droid bought by Watto—which can now barely see. Watto still hasn't figured out how the half-blind droid managed to walk into his shop in the first place.

While Anakin has tinkered with small devices for years, C-3PO is his first fully functional droid. Building a droid, even from standardized components, can be a challenge.

HIGH-TORQUE MOTOR

Rotating pin anchors into limb

Sturdy mount pole

MICRO-CIRCUIT WELDER

Welding stylus

Cleaner/ energizer

33

Blue color hints at Palpatine's interest in the Chancellorship

Elaborate cloak asserts sectorial authority

Senator Palpatine

ENDLESS PATIENCE has been Palpatine's key to success. Passed over as a young politician and repeatedly turned down for office and appointment, he has learned the value of quiet persistence. Palpatine has risen through the ranks to attain the powerful office of sectorial representative to the Galactic Senate on Coruscant. Palpatine represents some 36 worlds in a backwater sector, of which his provincial home planet of Naboo is typical. Turning this background to his advantage, Palpatine has been ever-present in the halls of galactic politics, impressing friend and opponent alike with his unassuming demeanor and simple but powerful insights into how the galaxy could be better run.

Over time Palpatine has developed a reputation as someone apart from intrigue and corruption, as he patiently condemns the many abuses of bureaucracy that come to his attention. It is no surprise to insiders that he is nominated for the office of Supreme Chancellor.

Palpatine's apartment is modest compared to the stunning palaces of other sectorial representatives

PALPATINE'S APARTMENT Few outsiders are welcomed into Palpatine's scarlet chambers. They are the exclusive haunt of his trusted confidants until Amidala arrives on Coruscant to plead her case.

Queen Amidala

Naboo-style bloused sleeves with long cuffs

Royal handmaiden

Strange red decor

Diplomat

Palpatine never favored Naboo's previous sovereign, King Veruna, even after the stubborn ruler heeded Palpatine's suggestions to become more involved in foreign affairs. Queen Amidala suits Palpatine, since he believes she will better follow his directions.

Before they meet at the Senate, Queen Amidala has only seen Palpatine in person once, at her coronation. She half-suspects that his concern for Naboo is secondary to his political ambitions.

DATA FILE

› Senator Palpatine's unusual choice of art objects reveals to Queen Amidala that he has left his Naboo heritage far behind and has adopted a more worldly point of view.

ROUTE TO SUCCESS Palpatine consistently favors less concern for senatorial legality and procedure and more attention to simply doing what he considers needs to be done. It is

as a result of this practical attitude that many look forward to the clear-minded leadership that Palpatine promises to provide.

The Senate
GALACTIC POWER

THE POWER of sectorial senators is immense, as they control access to the Senate for hundreds of planets. The temptations that go with such power are equally great. Corrupt senators are no longer unusual, even at the highest level, and few Republic citizens expect anything but empty promises and word games from anyone who sets foot on Coruscant. In truth, many senators are lazy and greedy, but by doing nothing to stop the spread of evil they become some of its greatest supporters.

Gesture showing objection

Gesture denying guilt

Gesture blaming others

Gesture of reassurance

MOT-NOT RAB

AKS MOE

PASSEL ARGENTE

HOROX RYYDER

SENATORIAL POLITICS
Many senators have become known for judicious nonalignment, allowing their worlds to profit from supplying both sides in conflicts. Critics comment that three-eyed Malastarians like Baskol Yeesrim can not only see both sides of an issue, but can always spot their position of advantage right in the center.

Ear flaps store fat

Lekku (head-tail)

Rare red-skinned Lethan Twi'lek

Consorts

Senators are attended by assistants, aides, and consorts according to customs and traditions of their home planets and sectors. Many young aides are repulsed by the abuses of government they see on Coruscant, but they stay on, reluctant to lose their positions of power.

Gaudy robe

Senator Tonbuck Toora's last traces of idealism have been eradicated by watching the downfall of the just and from counting the profits that flow from finding loopholes in the law. She now counts as friends criminal senators she once held in contempt and rewards loyal supporters with well-paid appointments as consorts or aides.

CONSORT TO TONBUCK TOORA

DATA FILE

> Lavender was chosen for the color of the Senate interior because it was the only hue that had never been associated with war, anger, or mourning in any culture in the Republic.

> Senator Tikkes moved from business to Coruscant politics to make some *real* money.

Senator Orn Free Taa

Indulgent lifestyles are nowhere more extreme than on Coruscant. Senator Orn Free Taa has found possibilities beyond his wildest dreams. He views galactic government as merely the sport of the mighty like himself. In his excesses, he has grown vile and corpulent, but he is confident that money and power will always make him attractive.

Flower of life emblem

Orichalc metal

NABOO CREST

Power transmitter

Magnetic turbine

Broadcast power receiver

COMLINK

Display can be keyed to scrambled Jedi transmissions

VIEWPAD

Setting for broadband or individual-specific signal

DROID CALLER

Standard cable hookup

BACKPACK POWER GENERATOR

Standard optical sighting scope

Handlock grip

STUN GUN

NABOO BLASTER

Nodule ridges distinguish slug from duracrete worm

Length 2.8 meters

Heavy handgrip for stability

Blade length adjust

Grip ridges

KI-ADI-MUNDI'S LIGHTSABER

DURACRETE SLUG

EPISODE II
ATTACK OF THE CLONES

IN A TIME OF INSTABILITY, the galaxy stands on the brink of rupture as powerful forces threaten to tear the Republic apart. The small numbers of peacekeeping Jedi cannot quell outright rebellion, and the great commercial powers are increasingly lured by the temptations of greed. Disruptive changes are at hand and the lines between good and evil are becoming unclear. Amid these epochal events, the galaxy's fate will turn upon the choices of only a few individuals, whose destinies are clouded. The Jedi have already lost a great leader with the defection of Count Dooku—will they now be forced to engage in the first full-scale war since the inception of the Republic? Where lies the path of honor in this uncertain time? When the valiant must choose between love and duty, peace and war, danger waits in every breath.

Trace in these pages the faces of legend, the shadows of inner turmoil, and the instruments of fate as one by one the final elements of a terrible destiny unfold.

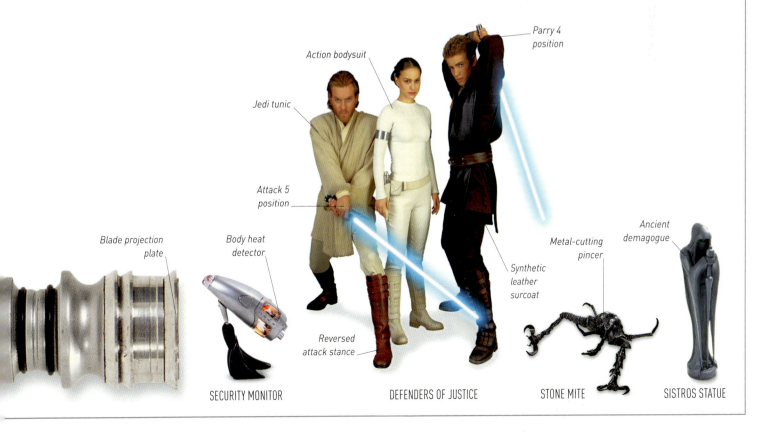

Blade projection plate

Body heat detector

Jedi tunic

Action bodysuit

Parry 4 position

Attack 5 position

Reversed attack stance

Synthetic leather surcoat

Metal-cutting pincer

Ancient demagogue

SECURITY MONITOR

DEFENDERS OF JUSTICE

STONE MITE

SISTROS STATUE

The Growing Darkness

LONG AGO, a prophecy foretold the coming of an individual who would "bring balance to the Force," ushering in a new era of peace following one of great instability. With the Separatist crisis, the future of the great Galactic Republic is clouded with uncertainty and the peace-keeping Jedi are too few to hold together an entire galaxy. In this age, the Sith have reappeared, their evil hidden perhaps in the heart of liberty's citadel—and while the prophecy is looked upon anew, many of the galaxy's denizens have no choice but to fend for themselves.

Beyond the vision of the Jedi Knights, somewhere within the darkness, the greatest master of evil ever to use Sith power bides his time. As his strength grows, his plans begin to shape the course of the galaxy, and his snares await the unsuspecting.

A Time of Change

Below the spires of Coruscant where the Jedi High Council and the Senate debate how to resolve the Separatist crisis, ordinary people struggle through a period of growing unrest. Ancient patterns are in upheaval and vast populations are on the move. In such a time, individuals must learn self-reliance and trust in what they can carry.

Twist-lock opens igniter housing

Muzzle guard

Charge cell

Cartridge housing

BLASTERS

Storage for gas, charge, and igniter cartridges

Reinforced pocket

CARTRIDGE POUCH

Pack holds samples of hot volcanic ore

PROBES

Reinforced covering

MESH GLOVES

Enhanced parallax sensors

Holographic display

SCANNER

Anti-microbe field plate

Antithermic frame

WATER POD

Accessory mount plate

Melt-proof Ceramoid mesh

Demagnetizing terminal

Anti-static tube

SCOUTER'S PACK

Heat dissipators

Module holds scouting information

Display screen

RECORD PAD

Discharge trigger

SURVIVAL OXYGEN

Zoom dial

Universal weatherproof housing

FOG SCOPE

Hidden Demons

Anakin Skywalker's fate has made him a Jedi and brought him to the center of events at the galactic capital. Senior Council members suspect he is the Chosen One. But like Coruscant itself, Anakin contends with inner demons against which an ancient prophecy seems little help.

Since its inception, the Republic has been protected by its system of law rather than by the force of armies. But the law is only as strong as its people, and when their vigilance fades, armies may regain the upper hand.

DATA FILE

› Many Coruscant freighters designed for hauling cargo are now forced by necessity to carry many hundreds of passengers as well.

› Military expenditures in the Republic are dramatically rising during this troubled period.

Jedi Padawan learner's braid reveals true identity to a Jedi initiate

Thousand Moons young matron's dress

Pattern common in Thousand Moons system

Private spire of Raith Seinar, military spacecraft engineering genius

Squad of clone troopers

Jedi boots in altered color

Refugees

Anakin Skywalker and the woman he is protecting flee Coruscant in disguise, but they cannot hide from the Sith. In the time of greatest crisis, they are caught within the plans of the powerful, and like all galactic refugees, find they must rely on their inner resources.

Severe hairstyle conforms to diplomatic etiquette

Neckband is gift from Naboo Council

Senator Padmé Amidala

AS ELECTED QUEEN of Naboo, Padmé Amidala won the lasting devotion of her people by showing extraordinary strength of character during the Trade Federation invasion. On the expiration of her second and final term of office, she yielded her authority in spite of popular demand for a change in the law that would have allowed her to rule longer. She was soon elected Senator to represent the 36 Naboo regional star systems; Padmé now travels widely to build support for her causes, returning to the galactic capital of Coruscant when necessary.

Senator Amidala's retinue returns to Coruscant in the sleek Naboo Cruiser to speak against a vote on the Military Creation Act. Padmé lands amidst high tensions and an invisible web of intrigue.

Cordé (disguised as Padmé)

Dormé

Like the Naboo Queen, Padmé is served and protected in vulnerable situations by loyal handmaidens who can act as decoys, assuming Padmé's identity.

Streamlined body for easy deployment from within garments

Naboo chrome finish

BLASTER

New tactical pilot suit

N-1 Camouflage

For security, Padmé sometimes travels disguised as a Naboo Starfighter pilot. Other planetary Senators would never condescend to yield the trappings of their status, so the simple ruse is effective.

Senatorial gown more low-key and practical than royal display garments Padmé wore as Queen

Auto-encrypting comm unit

Starfighter pilot emblem

Anti-glare goggles

Supplementary oxygen hookup

STARFIGHTER HELMET

Senatorial Dress

Padmé dresses with decorum when speaking in the Senate on important issues. A tireless champion of peace and freedom, she has worked for years against a much-debated proposal to create a great army of the Republic, which she believes might be the catalyst for war.

Senatorial Accommodation

While on Coruscant, Padmé and her retinue reside in quarters atop one of the ancient skyscrapers. Living in anything less than a penthouse would diminish Padmé's standing on the status-obsessed world and impede her diplomatic efforts. While the quarters are comfortable, Padmé loathes Coruscant's gray, artificial environment.

Padmé's apartment

Padmé's modest rooms do not have the fortress-like security systems used by more sophisticated politicians. When the Senator sleeps she is exposed to many unseen dangers.

UNTIMELY RETREAT
It takes two assassination attempts to convince Padmé to leave Coruscant for the safety of Naboo. Her retreat is a bitter one, for she will likely be absent during the vote on the army proposal and flight is alien to her character.

Subdued colors express grave mood

Synthetic leather gauntlets for hand-to-hand combat

Corset of light armor that doubles as protection

Traditional security tunic

Fabric hides uncomfortable blast-damping underskirt

Naboo blaster

Naboo military boots

Positive traction grip soles

Captain Typho oversees security for Senator Amidala and her retinue. He is the nephew of Captain Panaka, who served Padmé while she was Queen of Naboo.

Captain Typho

Raised to his Senatorial post because of his uncompromising loyalty and his ties to Panaka, Captain Typho is a relative novice to the world of lethal subterfuge that most galactic representatives in the Senate take for granted.

DATA FILE

› Naboo soldiers compose most of Captain Typho's security force on Coruscant.

› Captain Typho's eye patch is a mark of dedication, since he lost his eye in the line of duty.

Supreme Chancellor Palpatine

PALPATINE IS CAREFUL TO present himself as a mild-mannered servant of the public good, avoiding ostentation and ever protesting the limits of his abilities. Palpatine ascended to office amid mass frustration with the previous Supreme Chancellor—but there is increasing evidence that Palpatine himself quietly built much of this opinion behind the scenes. It also seems that a pattern may be emerging in Palpatine's work as Supreme Chancellor: Always citing the best interests of the Republic, he has consistently increased his own power, from legal authority to his institution of the Chancellor's Red Guard, who now attend every committee meeting. For some, his true intentions remain unclear.

Sleeves of ancient design

Subdued color and simple style convey gravity without pompous exhibitionism

Security Innovator

The Supreme Chancellor has placed the new Red Guard under his direct authority, while a Senatorial committee oversees the old Blue Guard. Palpatine calls this an efficient streamlining of cumbersome bureaucracy. Objectors have called it an illegal personal bodyguard, but such talk runs the risk of violating Palpatine's new security laws.

Although he prefers to avoid ostentation, Palpatine heeds the tradition for high political officials to maintain impressive audience chambers. During meetings, the large, scenic window reminds those involved that their decisions have wide repercussions.

Face shield protects Red Guard's identity

Blue Guard

Red Guard summoner

Hidden shield generator

Red Guard force pike

Ultra-dense lanthanide alloy armor

Blue Guard rifle

SEAT OF OFFICE
Palpatine has bowed to the concerns of his aides by accepting a special chair of office that affords him secret shielding and cunning protection. This chair also provides direct, secure communication with Palpatine's aides and with the Red Guard.

The Red Guard

Palpatine has kept the details of the Red Guard's training secret, citing security concerns. No one seems to know where this protection force and its trappings come from. Instead of stun rifles, the Red Guard use force pikes, which are more likely to be lethal.

Ceremonial stylings

Eyes see only in ultraviolet light

Umbaran shadowcloak is patterned in ultraviolet colors

Attack and display horns

Lethorns

The Jedi Council often discusses political opinions with Supreme Chancellor Palpatine. The support of the great Jedi reassures many who might otherwise doubt the Chancellor's motives.

Sly Moore and Mas Amedda

Sly Moore is Palpatine's Staff Aide. She controls access to the Chancellor, which gives her tremendous power. Moore comes from the shadowy world of Umbara, deep within the dark reaches of the Ghost Nebula. Umbarans are known for their abilities to subtly influence, and even control, others. As Speaker of the Senate, Mas Amedda is responsible for keeping order in debates.

He is a stern and stoic Chagrian, who refuses to comment on the changes he has witnessed during Palpatine's tenure.

While the average citizen has grown weary of politics, momentous events are afoot. Separatists foment unrest, and rumors are rife of secret armies. In ages past, safeguards limited the power of the Supreme Chancellor—but Palpatine calls them impediments to effective leadership, and may soon overturn them, with substantial support.

DATA FILE

> Palpatine's term ended several years ago, but a series of crises has allowed him to stay in office beyond the Senate's legal limit.

> Close aides say that Palpatine sometimes works for days without sleeping.

> Palpatine has revived the old tradition of appearing before the masses to accept their applause and vocal support.

OFFICE IDOLS
Palpatine's statues honor obscure figures from the past who possessed much arcane wisdom and law, but whose actions are shrouded in controversy.

HYPERDRIVE RING

Obi-Wan Kenobi
JEDI MENTOR

A DEDICATED JEDI KNIGHT facing a time of great crisis, Obi-Wan Kenobi finds himself at the heart of galactic turmoil as the Republic begins to unravel. Kenobi has witnessed the death of his Master, Qui-Gon Jinn, and knows the challenges the Jedi face in the defense of justice. He is cautious where his apprentice, Anakin Skywalker, is impulsive. Kenobi strives to train Anakin in the discipline that will make him a pillar of strength against the dark side. As dangers unfold, Kenobi's abilities and judgment form one of the last bulwarks against the collapse of the Republic.

SCANNER   COMLINK

Traditional leather utility belt

Lightsaber

Obi-Wan's Jedi apprentice is Anakin Skywalker, the boy suspected of being the prophesied individual who can "bring balance to the Force." Anakin's independence, born of his late induction into the Order, has brought Kenobi reprimands from Jedi elders Yoda and Mace Windu.

Trailing a would-be assassin into a nightclub on Coruscant, Kenobi steps casually to the bar "to have a drink." As planned, his apparent relaxation draws out his quarry, who finds that the Jedi's extraordinary powers give him a lightning edge—it is virtually impossible to take Obi-Wan by surprise.

Utility pouch

Food and energy capsules

Jedi tunic layered to adapt to different environments

Jedi robe

Rugged travel boots

DATA FILE

› The quartermasters in the Jedi Temple issue Obi-Wan with field equipment, such as this scanner monitor.

› Obi-Wan focused on Form III lightsaber training after the death of Qui-Gon Jinn.

Long hair of Jedi Knight

Two-handed grip for full saber control

Blade emitter

Blade modulation circuitry

Blade length and intensity control

Activator

Blade power adjust

Internal blade crystals

Handgrip

Power cell housing

Form III brace-ready stance

Kenobi specializes in Form III lightsaber combat, which maximizes defensive protection. Invented ages ago when blaster weapons first became common in the hands of Jedi enemies, Form III began as high-speed laserblast deflection training. Over the centuries, it has been refined into an expression of nonaggressive Jedi philosophy.

Piloting a Delta-7 starfighter on his field mission, Obi-Wan relies on a built-in Astromech Droid called R4-P17 to manage shipboard systems independently.

Captured on Geonosis, Kenobi comes face-to-face with Count Dooku, who once trained Qui-Gon Jinn. The Count tempts Obi-Wan with an offer of power in the Separatist regime, but Kenobi's dedication to justice is incorruptible.

Field Agent

Accomplished in a wide variety of skills ranging from diplomacy and psychology to military strategy and hand-to-hand combat, Obi-Wan has to be ready for anything on his field assignments. On Kamino, his investigation bursts into explosive conflict when bounty hunter Jango Fett resists arrest. Covered in armour and weaponry, Fett is a professional at the top of his field, but he cannot overcome Obi-Wan. The best Fett can manage is escape—with a powerful tracer beacon attached to his ship.

Signal port

TRACER BEACON

Star Tracker

Pursuing Jango Fett across the galaxy, Obi-Wan engages in a space duel with Fett and his deadly spacecraft, Slave I. Obi-Wan proves his abilities as an expert pilot and tactician, sacrificing his spare parts in a ruse to put Fett off his trail with apparent explosion debris.

From high in orbit, Obi-Wan's top-of-the-line starfighter sensor suite then traces Fett down to the weird planet surface of Geonosis.

Wide-band sensor scan

Sensor select monitor

Systems impedance monitor

STARFIGHTER DISPLAYS

Graphic damage monitor

Facing off against Count Dooku, Kenobi wisely exercises restraint where his apprentice rushes in headlong. A Jedi of powerful inner focus, Obi-Wan nevertheless finds he is unprepared for the Count's specialist techniques. Against Kenobi's Form III moves, the Count demonstrates the ancient and elegant precision of Form II lightsaber combat.

Anakin Skywalker
JEDI APPRENTICE

TWENTY-YEAR-OLD Jedi Padawan Anakin Skywalker is gifted with extraordinary Force skills and piloting abilities. His talents make him impatient with Jedi traditions that seem to hold him back and he often disagrees with the more cautious Obi-Wan Kenobi. Skywalker was accepted into the Order at the age of ten, far later in life than its rules allow, and his emotional bond with his mother was already strong. Anakin still struggles with the pain of this separation. Jedi Council members suspect Anakin of being the prophesied One who can bring balance to the Force. But Anakin must face ever steeper challenges to master the dangerous force that is himself.

Anakin is capable but not yet professional, criticizing his Master Kenobi in front of their charge, Senator Amidala. Anakin prefers to exceed his and Obi-Wan's mandate to only protect Padmé by trying to discover who is after her.

Padawan's short hairstyle with learner braid

Unconventional tunic color expresses Anakin's independence

Synthetic leather surcoat offers more protection than traditional cloth garment

Standard Jedi tunic style

Comlink pouch

Medical kit

Mechanical tool pouch

Food and energy capsules

LIGHTSABER

UTILITY BELT

Most Jedi Padawans build their lightsabers to resemble those of their Masters as a gesture of respect. Anakin constructed his own lightsaber while in a trance-like state, resulting in a design that favors maximum strength.

Heavy duty body cylinder

Activator and power indicator

Power-cell housing

Blue lightsaber blade generated via traditional Jedi crystals is more maneuverable but slightly less powerful than blade using synthetic Sith crystals

Synthetic leather protective boots

Field boots weighted for training

Dark Knight

The tunics, robes, and cloaks worn by Jedi are honored traditions, but not uniforms. From the time they become Padawans, Jedi are free to dress as they choose. Anakin Skywalker breaks with tradition in his garments, both in their color and material. His distinctive dark clothing makes him stand out at the Jedi Temple and draws concern from Jedi elders.

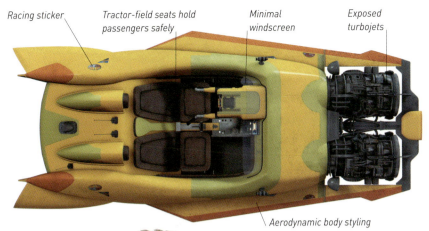

Racing sticker

Tractor-field seats hold passengers safely

Minimal windscreen

Exposed turbojets

Aerodynamic body styling

Airspeeder

Anakin is possibly the best pilot ever to train within the Jedi Temple. When he commandeers an airspeeder in pursuit of an assassin on Coruscant, his abilities are phenomenal. Anakin violates Jedi policies on vehicular speed and risk—guidelines intended to safeguard other craft, but not designed with so gifted a pilot in mind. Anakin's antics prompt the remark from Obi-Wan, "Why do I get the feeling you're going to be the death of me?"

Headdress disguise for Padmé

Forbidden Feelings

Only 20 Jedi have ever left the Order, but Anakin is coming perilously close. When he is assigned to protect the woman he has loved since childhood, he is torn between love and duty. The Jedi discipline does not seem to help him as it does the others, so his loyalties are put to the test: Will he insist on being an exception to the rules of the Jedi Order?

On Coruscant, Anakin suspects that Padmé has feelings for him. On Naboo, where Anakin's charm is in full force, Padme's feelings become transparent—but the inherent danger of their passions frightens both the Senator and the Jedi.

When Anakin senses his mother in terrible pain, Padmé goes with him to Tatooine in search of her. After Anakin fails to rescue Shmi in time, Padmé must alleviate the Padawan's anger, resentment, and despair.

In Anakin's mind, it is his own lack of resolve and strength that has failed his mother and caused him so much pain. At his mother's grave, marked by a black stone, Anakin makes a silent vow to build his strength until nothing can withstand his power.

Sensory impulse lines

Electromotive power lines

Interface module links wiring to nerves

Fingertips electrostatically sensitive to touch

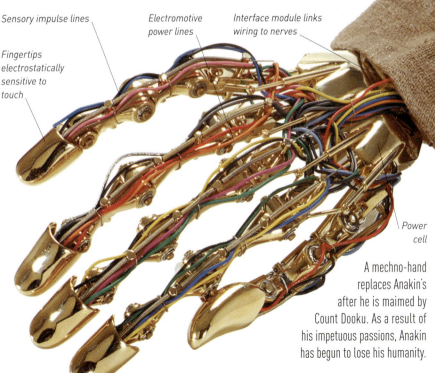

Power cell

A mechno-hand replaces Anakin's after he is maimed by Count Dooku. As a result of his impetuous passions, Anakin has begun to lose his humanity.

DATA FILE

> Anakin has started the study of lightsaber Form IV, known for its power.

> The pain of life-draining Sith lightning is an experience of evil that Anakin will never forget.

Zam Wesell

Scarf hides female humanoid visage

Subdued colors blend into building shadows

Stable two-handed aim

Direct-to-lungs breathpack

Hose fits grafted coupling in Zam's ribcage

Bodysuit stretches to allow shape-shifting

Elastic bands remain taut during body changes

Universal key

Blast-energy sink skirt

Shin-guard boots

Boots accept a variety of limb forms

AS A CLAWDITE SHAPE-SHIFTER, Zam Wesell can change her appearance to mimic a range of humanoid forms, giving her a special edge as a hired assassin. Zam learned her trade on Denon, the globe-girdling metropolis second only to Coruscant as a center of galactic business. In the high-risk world of industrial espionage, Zam rose from corporate security sergeant to executive bodyguard before seeking higher fees for contract execution and bounty hunting.

For some years Zam has worked on and off with renowned bounty hunter Jango Fett. Her latest job with Fett takes her to Coruscant, where Jango entrusts her with the assignment of killing a prominent Senator. Wesell knows that this opportunity will enhance her reputation and allow her to return to Denon as a master in her field.

ASN-121 ASSASSIN DROID

Bounty Hunter

A loner with few close associates, Zam Wesell is typical of bounty hunters. She inhabits a gray zone that extends to both sides of the law. Arrogant, highly skilled, and feeling unchallenged by legal bodyguard and security work, Wesell regards bounty hunting as a more suitable channel for her superior talent.

Stinger painful but not fatal

Bite delivers lethal nerve poison

KOUHUNS

Zam uses two deadly kouhuns for her Senatorial assassination job. Small, silent arthropods like the kouhuns of Indoumodo can evade even tight security. Unlike projectiles or energy weapons, they are virtually impossible to trace back to their users. Kouhuns are starved in advance, so they head straight for warm-blooded life forms when released, and use a fast-acting nerve toxin to kill their prey.

Mabari emblem

Third-level Mabari fighter markings

CAPE SEAL

Zam's discipline derives from the teachings of the Mabari, an ancient order of warrior-knights on her homeworld. She wears Mabari inscriptions and stylized emblems, including a cape seal that is an ancient Mabari artifact.

To prevent being traced, Zam Wesell prefers to steal a new vehicle for each new job. But when her security depends on performance she uses her own airspeeder.

Streamlined with enclosed cockpit for high speeds

Cleaning rod

Electromagnetic pulse barrel

Secret compartment for sniper rifle

Waste heat and radiation radiator

Zam favors her KYD-21 blaster pistol for both attack and defense, though Jango has begun teaching her that projectile weapons can be useful when working invisibly in the dark.

Blaster gas capsule loading port

Igniter pin

Hadrium alloy

Muzzle brake absorbs emitter flash

Embedding prongs

Injector needle

Guardless trigger for fast action

Poison chamber

Stabilizing fins

Handle holds power cell

KYD-21 Blaster

Though she carries a projectile rifle at Jango's insistence, Zam's primary weapon is a compact, precise KYD-21 pistol. She finds she can hide a pistol more easily when she needs to disguise herself as a non-threatening presence in order to close in on her mark.

Under intense Jedi mind-pressure, Zam begins to reveal her employer... until she is silenced by an assassin.

SABERDART
Preferring to leave no trace, Zam dislikes projectile weapons. A saberdart such as Jango might use may be silent and highly lethal, but has the potential to lead pursuers back to its source.

Light helmet

Visor cuts glare

Comlink system

Scrambled direct comlink pickup to Jango Fett

Clawdite shape-shifters, or "changelings," evolved on a world inhabited by warring humanoid subspecies. Shape-shifters developed the ability to mimic the appearance of other species in order to blend in without being killed. As a changeling dies, its ability to shape-shift fades and it returns to a neutral Clawdite configuration.

Flexible armorweave jerkin

High Stakes

Zam knows that in accepting a risky assignment from Jango Fett, she is in danger of being used as an expendable pawn. Such are the risks of the high-stakes trade in death, and Zam is prepared to take them... though she will find that she is not equipped to outrun two Jedi.

Simple optical scope

Power amplifier circuitry

DATA FILE
❯ Shape-shifting takes effort, and it is only through long practice that Zam has learned to rest in a mimicked form.

❯ Although shape-shifters are most effective at a limited range of shapes they imitate often, medical assistance can enhance their abilities much further.

Recoil-damping stock

PROJECTILE RIFLE

Jedi Temple

FOR MILLENNIA, the Jedi Temple on Coruscant has served as the training ground and home base of the Jedi Knights, peacekeeping defenders of justice throughout the galaxy. At the Temple, Jedi initiates learn the ways of the Force, a mystical energy field created by all living things. Hundreds of other individuals who are not Jedi Knights provide vital support in everything from operations management to technical analysis. The galaxy is so large that complete law enforcement is impossible; so most Jedi rove through assigned regions on "journey missions," empowered to support justice as they see fit. Jedi based at the Temple travel on special assignments.

The Jedi Temple on Coruscant occupies hallowed ground sanctified by the noble efforts of Jedi dating back many thousands of years into remote antiquity.

Jedi Padawan with learner braid

Traditional Jedi robes

The Jedi eschew materialism as they do any attachments that could cloud their judgment. Yoda's years of dedication have raised him to power and influence, but he meets his colleagues in a simple cell.

Natural skin coloration

Visually disruptive patterning

Active Jedi

Jedi begin their lifelong training when they are recognized as gifted children. They accept a life of total dedication and self-sacrifice to become diplomat-warriors. As initiates, they train together until they are accepted as Padawans, or apprentice learners. They must then face the Trials to become Jedi Knights, who are allowed in turn to take on an apprentice and earn the title of Master.

Gesture of patience

Diplomatic boots less rugged than field-agent boots

Shaak Ti

Jedi come from every corner of the galaxy. Jedi Master Shaak Ti is a Togruta, a species which lives in dense tribes on the planet Shili, where the disruptive coloration of their long lekku (head-tails) serves to confuse predators. Unlike most of her kind, Shaak Ti is a highly independent spirit.

Yoda—Jedi Instructor

THE WISE YODA is the sole member of the Jedi Council to recognize the present danger of Jedi complacency. Yoda sees that, in these troubled times, the greatest challenge may come from within the system itself. Even at his advanced age and with his formidable reputation and responsibilities, Yoda still trains young initiates. His students are taught to take nothing for granted and to keep their minds open to every possibility, avoiding the pitfalls of overconfidence.

Obi-Wan Kenobi has grown close to Yoda since the death of Kenobi's Jedi Master, Qui-Gon Jinn. Facing a difficulty in his current assignment, Obi-Wan does not hesitate to consult with his wise friend and colleague, who in turn uses the opportunity as an exercise for his young Jedi initiates.

Short Padawan haircut

Bear Clan member

Low-power "safety blade" generator

TRAINING LIGHTSABER

NOVICE HELMET
Young initiates wear helmets that mask their vision, training them to see using the Force rather than their bodily senses alone.

Adjustable-opacity faceplate

JEDI INITIATES

Sensitive ears complement Yoda's habit of listening more than talking

Hand gestures help focus mental use of the Force

Simple robe is a sincere expression of humility, despite Yoda's great power and reputation

Hidden Strengths

Yoda's capabilities with the Force give him amazing strength and speed, as well as the ability to levitate. These special powers, combined with his knowledge of fighting tactics, allow him to overcome virtually any opponent, though times are few indeed that Yoda has actually used his lightsaber in combat.

DATA FILE

› More than 9,000 fully trained Jedi are scattered throughout the galaxy, with a further 200 available at the Jedi Temple for emergency missions.

› Yoda has never revealed his homeworld, and his species is rarely seen anywhere in the galaxy.

Padmé—Naboo Senator

WHEN PADMÉ NABERRIE last saw Anakin Skywalker, he was just a boy, though she sensed something special about him even then. Now that Anakin has re-entered her life, Padmé is amazed at the effect the young Jedi has on her. She senses a connection that overcomes all her efforts to deny it, a feeling in conflict with her dedication and determination to serve her people. Her increasingly dangerous life and her exposure to the death of loved ones force Padmé to realize how precious every minute is. At the crucial moment, she becomes determined to live as fully as possible no matter what the consequences—and if she is to be destroyed, she will go down fighting.

Formal court hairstyle

After her years in political service, the planetary government complex on Naboo serves as a familiar walking place for Padmé.

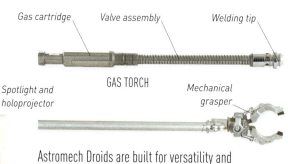

Padmé's family home in the Lake Country is called Varykino. It is here that she feels safest and can most be herself.

Processor status indicators

Camera eye

Spotlight and holoprojector

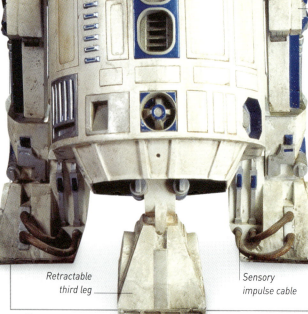

Retractable third leg

Sensory impulse cable

Gas cartridge *Valve assembly* *Welding tip*

GAS TORCH

Mechanical grasper

Astromech Droids are built for versatility and are easily fitted, and re-fitted, with a range of standardized parts and equipment.

Rocket assembly

Polydigital grasper

Actuator *Capacitor* *Extensor rod*

Symbol

All high offices on Naboo are elective, yet they carry with them the complex dress codes associated with hereditary nobility. Padmé accepts the symbolic value of such trappings but would prefer to wear clothes that express her own identity.

R2-D2

Padmé is faithfully attended by R2-D2, an Astromech Droid that regularly exceeds its programming in loyal service. While droids are disregarded through most of the galaxy, on open-hearted Naboo, Padmé is not unusual in feeling an affection for a mechanical servant who seems so spirited.

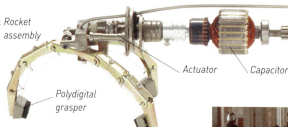

When Padmé returns from Coruscant, she consults with Queen Jamillia in Theed's Royal Palace. There, her old colleagues and political advisors struggle with small Naboo's surprisingly important role in the wider world of galactic politics.

Headband for decoration

Practical hairstyle for travel and action

Enhanced targeting-gear mounting bracket

Collimating tube and heat radiators

Military blaster

At Varykino, Padmé talks with Anakin about the difficult situation they face: Their demanding careers do not allow either of them to fall in love.

Trigger guard

Difficult one-handed grip

The Jedi and the Senator share their views on how galactic politics ought to run. Both are in positions to affect such matters.

Utility belt

Armband signifies political service

Individual

In her family home, Padmé is at last free to wear non-official clothing. Deeply affected by the presence of Anakin Skywalker, she tells herself that she cannot and will not fall in love with him, but unconsciously she wears a gown expressive of her true feelings.

Spare energy magazines for blaster

Customised H-type Nubian yacht

Pilot station

Padmé takes Anakin to Tatooine to help him find his mother, Shmi Skywalker. A decisive woman, she acts quickly when she realizes that time is short.

Fighter

Accompanying Anakin on his journey across the galaxy, Padmé plunges into the heart of the Separatist crisis. She faces extraordinary danger with the same determination that made her a successful Queen. Nothing can overcome her will.

After stepping down from the throne of Naboo, Padmé continues to use starships sheathed in regal mirrored chromium. The honor was awarded in respect of her pivotal role in repelling the Trade Federation's invasion of her planet.

DATA FILE

› Padmé served as Queen for the maximum two four-year terms and was elected Senator upon the conclusion of her reign.

› Padmé has had only limited weapons training but demonstrates natural skill at aiming a blaster.

› Free of the symbolic requirements of monarchy, Padmé can wear practical clothing on Geonosis.

Having survived great calamity together, Padmé and Anakin surrender to their feelings and marry. The marriage of a Jedi is a grave portent, violating a sacred code of honor in the Order.

Light shin armor

Action boots with firm grip

Kaminoans

WHEN A GLOBAL CLIMATE SHIFT flooded their planet, the Kaminoans were forced to adapt. They developed cloning technology and practised selective breeding to keep their race alive. As a result of the hardships endured during the Great Flood, the Kaminoans have an austere, non-materialist outlook. They are outwardly polite, yet behind this lurks an extreme intolerance of physical imperfection.

The Kaminoans are reliant on certain outworld technologies and raw materials to maintain their advanced society, so they use their cloning abilities to produce goods for export. When a Jedi named Sifo-Dyas placed an order for a massive clone army a decade ago, the Kaminoans embarked upon the largest human cloning project ever undertaken.

Female Kaminoans lack headcrest

Large eyes see well in murky conditions

KO SAI

Elongated bones allow limited flexibility in neck

TAUN WE

Long neck consists of seven elongated bones

The planet Kamino once had extensive land areas, but the melting of inland continental glaciers sank all land beneath the waves. Today, only the Kaminoan stilt cities project above the water, forming colonies of varying sizes around the planet.

Black body-glove underlayer

Clone science emblem

Clone serum test probe

Serum sample pouch

Black cuff is a mark of honor; scientific rank indicated by thickness

Spongy wings

Kaminoans use domesticated aiwhas for sport and transportation between close-sited colonies. These animals can fly and swim with equal ease, controlling their density using a water-vascular system. This system allows the aiwhas to fill their spongy tissues with seawater when they want to swim underwater, and to wring the water out and shed it to lighten themselves for flight.

Kaminoan saddle rig

Skull contains buoyancy chambers

Sieve plates filter plankton underwater or in flight

Obi-Wan Kenobi identifies himself as a Jedi to Kamino Space Traffic Control on his way in and, upon landing, is met by the Prime Minister's assistant.

Project Leaders

Dexterous fingers

Ministerial assistant Taun We serves as a Project Coordinator for the clone army. Taun We has studied human emotional psychology to ensure that the clones are developed into mentally stable individuals. Chief Scientist Ko Sai, serene yet exacting, oversees the clone-army project's biological aspects, ensuring that clones are of the highest quality. She also supervizes the delicate redesign of the genetic codes that make the clones independently intelligent, but preconditioned for obedience. No other scientist in the galaxy could so capably manipulate the genes of another species.

White form-fitting clothing

Cloak of office

Kamino's prime minister, Lama Su, is well aware of the clone army's importance to his economy. He personally meets the Jedi whom he thinks has come to inspect it.

Lama Su is unsure whether Obi-Wan Kenobi's seeming ignorance of the tremendous clone army is a devious test or a complex form of politeness. Regardless, his main concern in meeting with Kenobi is to ensure that the Kaminoans will obtain their first shipment bonus payment, so he makes nothing of the Jedi's behaviour.

Kaminoan stilt cities echo the Kaminoans' former land colonies. These were communal dwellings constructed of wattle and daub, which shed water easily in the long storm seasons.

DATA FILE

> Kaminoans see color only in the ultraviolet spectrum. Their seemingly white dwellings are suffused in many shades that humans cannot see.

> Prime Minister Lama Su is the head of the ruling council of Kamino colony governors. He is aware of the larger arena of galactic events, but is nonetheless little interested in outworld politics.

Digitigrade configuration of feet adds height

Small feet adapted to firm Kaminoan seabeds and now to hard flooring

TIPOCA (KAMINOAN CAPITAL CITY)

Communications tower

Static discharge towers vital during electrical storms

Streamlined outer shell sheds water and wind

Pylons present minimal silhouette to avoid wave battering

Pylons embedded in shallow continental shelf below

Clone Trooper Growth

CLONE ARMY
PROJECT
EMBLEM

THE MYSTERIOUS Jedi Sifo-Dyas ordered from the Kaminoan cloners a secret army created from a single individual. An agent named Tyranus selected the clone-source: Jango Fett, a man whose natural combat ability and high endurance level would produce the ideal soldier. Under Kaminoan Chief Scientist Ko Sai, the clones' genetic code was altered to accelerate their growth to twice the normal human rate, and their mental structure was subtly reconfigured to make them obedient to authority. Comprehensive training shapes the identity and abilities of the clones throughout their development. The result of this colossal project is an army of identical soldiers produced in a world of clinical efficiency.

Most Kaminoans regard the clones as laboratory specimens but Taun We feels some affection for the young cadets.

The clones begin life as artificially created embryos that are mass-produced in the Egg Lab.

Odd-class helmet has gold plating

Broadcast power receiver

Anodized-color equipment for even-class helmet

Broadcast signal receiver

Durable inert plastoid helmet

EVEN-CLASS HELMET

Mental receptivity enhancer

ODD-CLASS HELMET
The clones wear special learning helmets, which are color coded to reflect odd or even numbering. Odd or even is the only identity distinction the clones are allowed.

Biorhythm synchronizer

Earphone silences external sounds to provide isolated audio environment for learning

Accelerated Learning

Clone youths grow at twice the rate of ordinary humans, so they crave information but receive only half the normal time to assimilate it. This loss of life-experience is compensated for by a learning program that focuses more on military knowledge than on academics. In addition, special equipment modulates brainwaves and enhances the clones' ability to retain instruction.

Pickup reads vocal responses

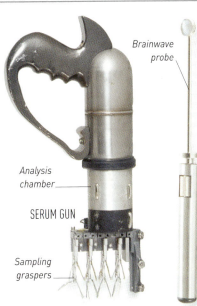

Brainwave probe

Brainwave canceler

Analysis chamber

SERUM GUN

Sampling graspers

Reorientation unit

Clone birth pod

Maintaining Perfection

The Kaminoans strive to control every aspect of the clones' existence for perfect regularity, but slight deviations occur in the development of any living individual's biochemistry. Chief Scientist Ko Sai inspects the clones at every stage of life to identify those who have drifted from the standard. Aberrant clones are given extra conditioning to regularize them.

Blank character and accelerated growth shape clone face slightly differently from clone-source

Utility garments in security bicolor style

Cord used for symbolic honor training

The Kaminoans' dedication to perfection has led to methods of absolute sterilization and ultraclean surfaces so the clones are not in any way tainted with imperfections. Such standards are extraordinary for so vast an enterprise, and Obi-Wan Kenobi is astonished.

Batches of clones are trained in an environment with exactly enough semblance of community to make them emotionally stable. Physical skills are imparted through learning devices and are perfected through practice.

Developed Clone

The stress of accelerated physical, mental, and emotional growth could easily drive a clone insane. To counter this and produce sound soldiers, the Kaminoans provide a highly disciplined environment and a rigorously balanced development program. At a physical age of just ten years, the clones are fully developed and ready for battle, though they cannot be said to have normal personalities.

Loose cut allows physical training without changing attire

As "adults," the clone troopers resemble their source, Jango Fett. Fett lives on Kamino and helps train the troopers, knowing better than anyone how to guide their development and impart military skills to the copies of himself.

DATA FILE

❯ The Kaminoan cloners recondition an average of seven aberrants for every two hundred clones produced, maintaining superb standards.

❯ Ordinary soldiers might become claustrophobic when sealed into armor, but clone troopers are trained to wear it for extended periods.

Clone Trooper Equipment

CLONE TROOPER armor and equipment is based in part on the battle gear of the Mandalorian "shocktrooper" supercommandos, of whom Jango Fett is a survivor. Fett's light armor inspired the heavy-duty shell completely covering the clone trooper. Replacing the Mandalorian flightsuit is a pressurized black body-glove that protects against acrid vapors or even the vacuum of space. The distinctive shocktrooper "T" visor plate is adapted with an enhanced breath filter for optimal operations under the often poor environmental conditions of battle. Together with their superb training and conditioning, clone troopers feel virtually invincible with this panoply.

DC-15 Blaster

Outfitted in their extraordinary gear, clone troopers can withstand hails of deadly projectiles or explosive blasts with impunity. They are also able to march through deflector shield barriers that would incinerate even a shocktrooper.

Spare blaster igniters

Stock contains powder-charge magazine

Gas release valve

Utility belt carries spare blaster magazines, survival gear, and assault equipment

Thigh plate

Nonconducting stock

Gas cartridge safety lock

Pressurized blaster gas cartridge

Gas pressure indicator

Tibanna gas, highly charged and pressurized

Magnatomic adhesion grip

Body Armor

Clone trooper body armor is made of 20 form-fitting plates of lightweight plastoid-alloy composite. Troopers receive and send battle status signals via communication equipment contained in their helmets. Fabricated by an alien species with a limited knowledge of human ergonomics, the armor allows reasonable freedom of movement in combat, but is uncomfortable to sit in when troopers pilot vehicles. Future versions and upgrades of this body armor will undoubtedly include improvements in this respect.

Plates seal onto body-glove via magnatomic gription panels

Armor aesthetic displays Kaminoan influence in its stark scheme

High-traction soles

DATA FILE

> As the clone-source for the entire clone-trooper army, Jango Fett cooperated in devising the design of the armor, based on his combat experience.

> Republic assault ships transport the gunships that deploy clone troopers under heavy fire protection.

Enhanced breath filter for battle conditions

Comlink antenna built into helmet

Laser turret

Heavy-lift agrav drive

AT-TE

Armored hull

REPUBLIC GUNSHIP

AT-TE CARRIER

"T" visor derived from shocktrooper helmet

All-terrain walking legs

AT-TE WALKER

Spare blaster magazine

Grappling hook

Knee plate

WHITE TERROR
Clone trooper uniforms are not camouflaged, because troops fear no one and want their enemies to see them coming from afar.

Battle Gear

Vital combat transports and fighting machines have been developed alongside the clone troopers. This new equipment expresses the battle philosophy of the clone army: It is built for heavy use and the unleashing of maximum-effort assaults without warning. These approaches differ from the forms of battle seen throughout the galaxy for thousands of years, in which armies deployed their strength cautiously over long periods.

Troop deployment hatch (raised)

Command bridge

Walking legs

SPHA-T

Power amplifier circuitry

Expansion chamber

Power setting adjust

Galven circuitry

Collimating tube

Flip-up optical sight for open combat

Ignition chamber

Electromagnets

Igniter

Accelerator

Pre-ionizer

Heat-exchange elements

Radiator fins

Hyper-ionizer

Weaponry

Heat radiator fins

Magnetic pulse stabilizers

Rifle break point for replacement of gas cartridge

Sniper scope in storage position doubles as handhold

DC-15 RIFLE

Weighted stock improves balance of rifle

Clone troopers are issued plasma guns of two types. Like all standard blaster weapons, these guns create a charged plasma bolt using a small amount of Tibanna gas. Blaster weapons free clone troopers from the need to carry projectile ammunition but are notoriously hard to aim due to the inherent instability of plasma bolts.

Heat exchange elements in muzzle reduce danger of damage from overheating

Charge magazine locks in on opposite side

Heavy duty fasteners

Tibanna gas is carried in a replaceable cartridge that lasts about 500 shots, depending on the weapon's settings and traits. Power-charge magazines supply the gun with energy to hyper-ionize the gas into charged plasma in an igniter chamber. The resulting bolt is accelerated out of the gun electromagnetically.

Charge magazine

Spare igniter

DC-15 BLASTER

Lock-in charge magazine

Blaster lacks rifle's enhanced power control components, limiting range

Folding stock for braced firing

Jango Fett—Bounty Hunter

AFTER THE MURDER of his parents, Jango Fett was adopted and raised by the legendary Mandalorian warrior army, a mercenary group who earned a reputation as the most formidable supercommandoes in the galaxy. The Jedi destroyed this dangerous force, but Fett survived and continues to wear the armored, weapon-filled uniform that helped make the Mandalorians a dreaded name. Keeping himself in top condition and training often with his equipment, Jango Fett combines physical and tactical skill with a prudent intelligence that is a rare attribute in the bounty-hunting community.

Jango's reputation enables him to hire stringers, wisely minimizing his own risk. He often works with Zam Wesell, to whom Jango assigns the dangerous job of assassinating the Senator for Naboo.

Explosive/grappling missile

Fuel tank

Gauntlets can mount various weapon systems

Jetpack

Jetpack activator

Gimbaling servo

Rocket thrust vectoring nozzle

Segmented armor plate allows flexibility

Traditional sash binding of journeyman protector

Holster design holds and protects custom-made pistols

Waterproof layered flight suit

Tactical boots with magnatomic adhesion soles

Kneepad rocket-dart launchers

Pineal eye sensor allows Jango to see behind him

Helmet design balances protection with tactical visibility

WESTAR-34 blaster

Gauntlet projectile dart shooter

Whipcord thrower

Utility pouches

Even the surprise appearance of a Jedi Knight is not enough to overcome Fett's topnotch combat skills. When Obi-Wan Kenobi tries to capture him, Jango is well-prepared and instantly launches a volley of blasts that would annihilate an ordinary opponent.

In battle with Kenobi, Fett soon appreciates the seemingly supernatural abilities of the Jedi. Jango must quickly re-assess his tactical situation before Kenobi gains the upper hand.

Walking Armor

Mandalorians who could afford it commissioned backup suits of their armor. Fett has replacement armor for much of his suit, with additional items that can be fitted for particular mission profiles. Some configurations stress brute-force armament, while others maximize nonlethal weapons used for capturing quarry.

Ultrasonic emitter

FIELD SECURITY OVERLOADER

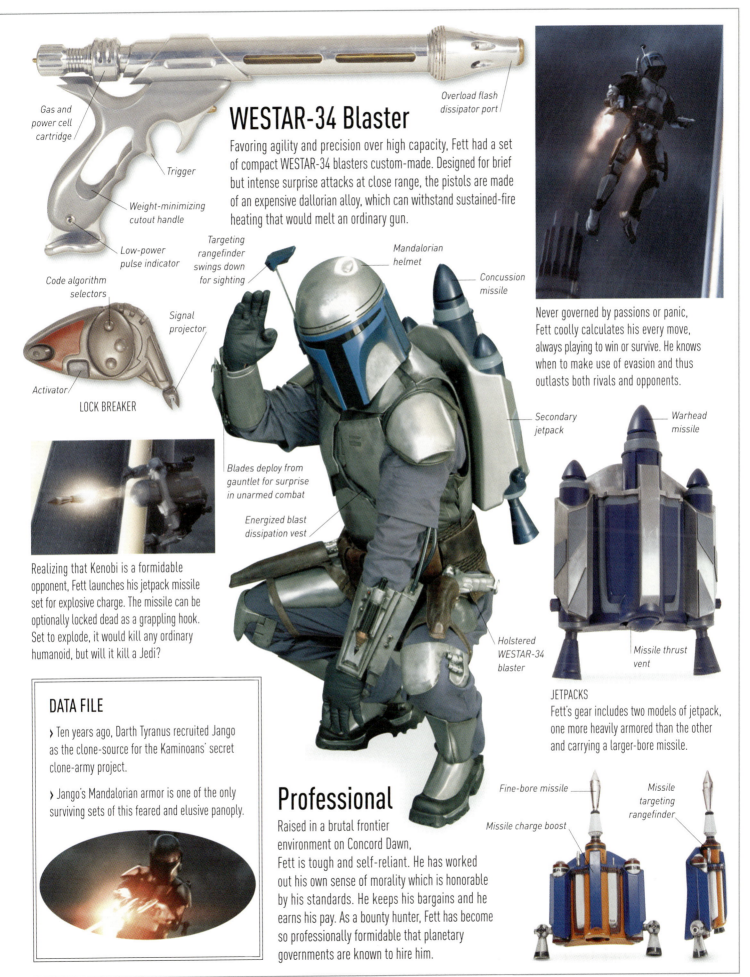

WESTAR-34 Blaster

Gas and power cell cartridge

Trigger

Weight-minimizing cutout handle

Low-power pulse indicator

Overload flash dissipator port

Favoring agility and precision over high capacity, Fett had a set of compact WESTAR-34 blasters custom-made. Designed for brief but intense surprise attacks at close range, the pistols are made of an expensive dallorian alloy, which can withstand sustained-fire heating that would melt an ordinary gun.

Code algorithm selectors

Signal projector

Activator

LOCK BREAKER

Never governed by passions or panic, Fett coolly calculates his every move, always playing to win or survive. He knows when to make use of evasion and thus outlasts both rivals and opponents.

Targeting rangefinder swings down for sighting

Mandalorian helmet

Concussion missile

Secondary jetpack

Warhead missile

Blades deploy from gauntlet for surprise in unarmed combat

Energized blast dissipation vest

Realizing that Kenobi is a formidable opponent, Fett launches his jetpack missile set for explosive charge. The missile can be optionally locked dead as a grappling hook. Set to explode, it would kill any ordinary humanoid, but will it kill a Jedi?

Holstered WESTAR-34 blaster

Missile thrust vent

JETPACKS
Fett's gear includes two models of jetpack, one more heavily armored than the other and carrying a larger-bore missile.

DATA FILE

❯ Ten years ago, Darth Tyranus recruited Jango as the clone-source for the Kaminoans' secret clone-army project.

❯ Jango's Mandalorian armor is one of the only surviving sets of this feared and elusive panoply.

Professional

Raised in a brutal frontier environment on Concord Dawn, Fett is tough and self-reliant. He has worked out his own sense of morality which is honorable by his standards. He keeps his bargains and he earns his pay. As a bounty hunter, Fett has become so professionally formidable that planetary governments are known to hire him.

Fine-bore missile

Missile charge boost

Missile targeting rangefinder

The Lars Family

Settler's simple hairstyle

Rough clothing made in Anchorhead

Tunic

Desert robe

TATOOINE'S moisture farmers survive in territories most other people consider uninhabitable. In their search for an independent existence away from the overcrowding and often slave-like employments of the Core Worlds, the Lars family have made Tatooine's barren desert their home. Rendered close-knit by the dangers and hardships they all face, the Lars family and the moisture-farming community band together against the native Tusken Raiders. Pioneer settler Cliegg Lars earned his farm by a homestead claim, raising his son Owen on the great salt flats, together with his second wife, a former slave named Shmi Skywalker.

MUSHROOM JAR

Moisture farms on the salt flats of Tatooine use arrays of vaporator towers spread out across vast distances to extract minute amounts of water from the atmosphere. A precious commodity on the desert world, water can be used for barter, for sale, or for hydroponic gardens. Homesteads are dug into the ground to provide respite from extreme temperatures.

Owen never expected to meet his step-brother, Anakin, knowing that Jedi must sever their family ties. When Anakin arrives, Owen has mixed feelings about his more worldly relation who left his own mother to become a Jedi.

Owen and Beru

The small town of Anchorhead provides a nexus for the moisture-farming community of the Great Chott salt flat. There, Owen Lars met Beru Whitesun, his girlfriend. Beru's family have been moisture farmers for three generations, making them among the settlers most thoroughly adapted to Tatooine life.

The Lars' kitchen is a simple, functional space built around the basic concern of conserving moisture. Food is never left out for long, and moisture traps are built into the self-sealing cabinets.

DATA FILE

> Owen Lars was born to Cliegg Lars and his first wife Aika before Cliegg left the Core World of Ator.

> The Lars family maintains an array of some 63 water vaporators spread out across the flat desert around the homestead, making their farm a relatively small one by Tatooine standards.

C-3PO

Anakin Skywalker built the working skeleton of C-3PO out of scrounged droid parts when he was just a boy and still a slave. Two years after her son's departure, Shmi Skywalker acquired a set of old droid plating from her then master, Watto. Shmi installed the plates to help the droid last longer in the sandy environment.

Enhanced vision spots circuitry damage

Sub-par droid plating

Flexible unplated midsection

Power and impulse wiring

Salvaged metal from transport container

Control stick

Power unit

Repulsor coils

Mostly sandproof joint

Cliegg Lars

Cliegg Lars left behind life in a cramped garret within a centuries-old Core World skyscraper to run a farm on Tatooine. Looking for a farmhand, instead he found a woman whom he fell in love with. In order to marry Shmi, he bought her freedom from Watto, the junk dealer.

Improvised protective gear

Most settlers have no blasters

When Shmi Skywalker is kidnapped by Tusken Raiders, a posse of moisture farmers go in search of her. But these peaceable folk are little prepared to face the savagery of Tusken Raiders.

Activator

Mechno-Chair

When Tusken Raiders ambush the nearly defenseless settlers who attempt to rescue Shmi, Cliegg Lars' leg is cut off by a lethal trick-wire. Refusing to be fitted with a mechno-leg, Cliegg is confined to a power chair.

Induction drives

Footrest

Homemade blaster

Overheat radiators

Power cell

Discarded ignition chamber

Simple laser sight

Stun blast nozzle

SETTLER WEAPONS
The few weapons available to the impoverished settlers are low-powered blasters.

Facing Loss

After the Tusken tragedy, some wonder whether the moisture farming community will be abandoned. With the death of Shmi, Cliegg Lars has lost as much as anyone, yet he remains determined to live out the life he has worked so hard to create.

Count Dooku

THE DANGEROUS AND ELEGANT Count Dooku was once a Jedi Master of great repute. He left the Jedi Order after the Battle of Naboo, returning to his homeworld of Serenno and his family title of Count. By protesting the failure of galactic government, Dooku has swayed many systems to the Separatist movement, which seeks independence from the Republic, but his real motives lurk in darkness. The Count has always wielded considerable power—by natural authority, by lightsaber, and now by wealth and persuasion. This double-dealing master of the Force has taken a place at the heart of galactic events and he threatens the very survival of the Republic.

Count's gaze immobilizes weak-minded individuals

In the droid foundries of Geonosis, the Count hopes to have found the anvil upon which he can forge the sword of the Republic's undoing.

Cape is emblem of Count of Serenno

Curved lightsaber hilt allows precise crossparry moves

Cape enlarges Count's silhouette to intimidating effect

Dark Alignment

Although Dooku joined the Order at the usual age, he never fully gave it his inmost allegiance. He maintained a streak of independence, which he transmitted to his pupils, including the late Qui-Gon Jinn. Dooku's considerable strength in the Force made him enigmatic even to Yoda, and there were whispers that he experimented with Sith teachings, using a dark Holocron kept in the Jedi Archives. The Council underestimated Dooku's interest in power.

Underlayer made of costly, fine-grade armorweave fabric, which drapes like silk and helps dissipate blast or lightsaber energy

Elegant, tall dress boots

DATA FILE

› The Count is master of his family's fortune and one of the wealthiest men in the galaxy. He could field an army on his own resources.

› As a youngling, Dooku trained under Yoda. The great Jedi Master hoped, with careful teaching, to overcome the effects of Dooku's persistent independent spirit.

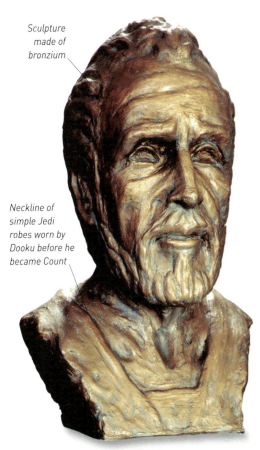

Sculpture made of bronzium

Neckline of simple Jedi robes worn by Dooku before he became Count

Dooku's Lightsaber

As a Jedi Master, Count Dooku set aside the lightsaber he built as a young Padawan and created a superior one, as Jedi sometimes do. In creating his personalized design, he chose a configuration that had no connection to that of his master, Yoda, nor to the style in fashion at the time. Instead, he studied Jedi Archives records to create a lightsaber of the type that was standard in the heyday of Form II lightsaber combat. Form II is an ancient technique that favors long, elegant moves and incredible deftness of hand.

Emitter guard

Thumb trigger can shorten blade instantly for short-range surprise attack

Thermal radiator grooves

Blade emitter

Inclined blade focusing chamber

Dooku tempts the captured Obi-Wan Kenobi with an offer to join him in the Separatist movement. The Count subtly uses the Force to probe Obi-Wan's spirit for inner weaknesses.

Sith synthetic crystals (inside saber) replace original ones for greater power

The Lost Twenty

Only 20 individuals in the history of the Jedi Order have ever renounced their commissions. Their leave-taking is sorely felt among the Jedi, who memorialize them with portrait busts in the Archives. Count Dooku is the most recent of the "lost" ones. He is considered the most bitter loss because the Force was so strong in him.

The curved hilt of Dooku's lightsaber allows for superior finesse and precise blade control. This design gives Dooku an edge when facing Jedi, who have mostly trained to use lightsabers to deflect blaster bolts.

Projector

Cells given by Sith Master

HOLOPROJECTOR
After he left the Jedi Order, Dooku was no longer able to use the Sith Holocron in the Archives. He now studies holographic cells containing mystic teachings of shadowy power.

When the arrival of the Jedi forces spoils his primary plans, Dooku uses one of his several means of escape—a small, open-cockpit speeder bike.

Activator

Magnatomic adhesion plates

Dooku reveals the full measure of his dark nature when he casts legendary Sith lightning. Virtually impossible to deflect, Sith lightning causes excruciating pain and weakens life. The Jedi possess no exact equivalent to such an evil use of the Force.

Fastener

Reserve power cell

Compound power cell

Phase A power cell

The Separatists

COUNT DOOKU'S CALL for independence from the decaying and increasingly corrupt Republic is answered by some of the most significant and authoritative factions in the galaxy. Among them stands a sinister gathering of commercial empires and megaconglomerates, whose power could rival that of the Republic itself. Disaffected and opportunistic Senators also support the Separatist movement. The political system was never constructed to deal with the rise of corporate superpowers, whose motives and morals focus on profit alone. Without decisive support from the Galactic Senate, the Republic's very structure is in danger of being undermined.

The Corporate Alliance

The Corporate Alliance is the negotiating body for the galaxy's major commercial operations. As head of the largest corporation, Passel Argente commands the office of Alliance Magistrate. Argente has risen to great heights of wealth and power as chairman of the merchandising conglomerate called Lethe. Workers and consumers are encouraged to identify with the company in a near-religious way.

RUNE HAAKO

Large, pompous miter

Conniving gesture

NUTE GUNRAY

Elaborate Neimoidian headdress

Oath-taking gesture

Sign of insincerity

Command control reception antenna

Tracking transmitter

Stereoscopic visual sensor

Drive axis hub

Weapons outrigger

High-traction drive tread

Stabilizing outrigger

Robust male cranial horn

PASSEL ARGENTE

Oily cloak

Grasping hands

CORPORATE ALLIANCE TANK DROID
When Alliance corporations face resistance to their development plans, Tank Droids are used to clear the way. The wheel-like machines are widely feared.

The Trade Federation

The Trade Federation controls freighters, ports, and way stations on the galactic commerce routes. Its power is profitably supported by a droid army, which operates under the guise of "securing the lines of trade." Trade officials appear immune to prosecution for their brutal intimidation.

Communications tower

TRADE FEDERATION CORE SHIP
Large Trade Federation freighters are not designed for planetary landings. However, the core ships can detach from the freighters and descend on their own.

The Commerce Guild

The Commerce Guild seeks to control any large corporation involved in raw materials. Increasingly, it enforces tribute payments with its private army. The Guild maximizes profit by stifling alternative technologies and bribing corrupt officials and Senators to control market forces with tariffs.

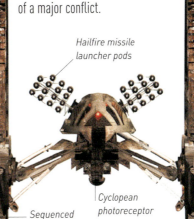

Traditional skullcap

Gossam rings elongate neck

HOMING SPIDER DROID

Armored body core

Extension hydraulics

All-terrain legs

PRESIDENT SHU MAI

Gracile female cranial horn

Homing laser

Parallax signal tracing dish

Ambulation motors

Tracing antenna

Koorivan matron's hood

Infrared photoreceptor

DENARIA KEE (AIDE)

Formal breastplate of office

DWARF SPIDER DROID
Commerce Guild army droids are built with striding legs for roadless terrain on rugged mining worlds. These destructive droids hunt down operations attempting to evade tribute payments.

Subservient gesture

Robe made of shimmerbird tongues

The IG Banking Clan

The InterGalactic Banking Clan is headquartered on Muunilinst. It is vastly powerful, with most influence shared by a few old banking families. The fiscally prudent chairman San Hill views the galaxy in purely monetary terms, so he naturally finances both sides of a major conflict.

Palo Banking garb

Pale skin from indoor living

SAN HILL

Hailfire missile launcher pods

Hoop wheel

HAILFIRE DROID
Hailfire Droids roll rapidly into action to discourage those who might default on IG Banking Clan loans. Murderous explosive missile launchers dispatch "late payment notices."

Sequenced magpulse drive

Cyclopean photoreceptor

PO NUDO   AIDE

Shi'ido changeling in disguise

Food manipulation tentacles

Large aural chamber

TIKKES

Senators

Demoralized by bureaucratic inaction and corruption, some Senators see Count Dooku's bid for independence as a brave and noble cause. Others align themselves with the Separatists merely for greater personal gain.

DATA FILE

> Count Dooku leads the Separatists and knows every faction's weak points.

> Most commercial armies are legally licensed even though they violate the spirit of the laws against private armies.

Trade Federation Battle Droids

THE WEALTHY TRADE FEDERATION is a key faction in the Separatist movement, supplying its army of Battle Droids. The Trade Federation's defeat in the Battle of Naboo made clear the need for stronger, more independent infantry forces, and thus the Super Battle Droids were commissioned as improvements on their standard, skeletal-form predecessors. Like the terrifying droideka, these military-grade robots violate Republic regulations on private security forces, but the Neimoidians have too much influence to fear the galactic courts. Count Dooku himself arranged the deal in which a large force of Super Battle Droids are being secretly manufactured within the droid foundries of Geonosis, building even greater power for the Separatists.

Standard Trade Federation Battle Droids are still in use, having proven effective at policing subject populations.

Heavy shoulder armor protects command signal receptor

Main signal receptor unit buried in reinforced armor

Arms stronger than Battle Droid limbs

Thick acertron armor protects primary power unit in chest

Neimoidians are too fearful to fight their own battles and too deceitful to trust living soldiers, preferring to use Battle Droids for their nefarious purposes. Often criticized for their cowardliness, they have found Count Dooku surprisingly supportive of their mechanized army.

Super Battle Droid

The tough and durable Super Battle Droid's armor and reinforced joints sacrifice some mobility for improved protection. For economy, the design makes use of standard Battle Droid internal components, but packages them in a much stronger shell.

Enhanced signal receptor package

Broad areas most heavily armored

Dehumanized silhouette increases intimidation effect

Limbs remain narrow in forward silhouette for target minimization

High center of gravity balanced by movement algorithms

Flexible armored midsection

Cryogenically-tempered body-shell elements are hardened, but flex slightly under stress to reduce breakage

DATA FILE

➤ The droidekas' superior construction and design explains their high cost, which is over 200 times the price of a Battle Droid.

➤ Unlike droidekas, humans cannot carry personal shield generators because of the technology's high radioactivity.

Heavy droideka can project its own defensive shield

Complex form can fold up into a ball shape for movement to battle site

Custom-made blaster units use high-pressure blaster gas

Handtip contains firing impulse transmitter to trigger standard blaster weapons

Blaster hands built only for battle

Droideka

Heavy-duty droidekas are invulnerable to standard blaster weapons and Jedi lightsabers. These fearsome and illegal assault robots have been known to blast even their owners if not perfectly operated. Neimoidian lawyers have helped the Colicoid manufacturers of the droideka evade costly death and damage lawsuits.

Recess on hidden inner surface to reduce weight

High-torque motors

Firing impulse generators

Excess heat radiated through calf vanes

Shinplate hard-forged in one piece

Reinforced ankle joint

Strap-on foot tips can be replaced with claws or pads suited to different terrain

Monogrip hands lack dexterity but are hard to damage

Knee joint bearings hermetically sealed

Jedi in Battle

JEDI KNIGHTS use their powers of subtle perception to resolve conflicts through negotiation and diplomacy. They seek peace through justice, knowing that true harmony can rarely be forced upon a situation. Nonetheless, mystical philosophy has never blinded the Jedi to the practical need for force in intractable situations, and the most studied Jedi diplomats are capable of drawing their lightsabers in an eyeblink when crisis demands it. When war preparations are discovered on Geonosis, Mace Windu is quick to act, leading a Jedi expedition of all available fighters to rescue Obi-Wan Kenobi.

Pullback for cutting sweep

Horizontal parry

Different tentacles detect specific chemical signatures

Kit Fisto

As an amphibian Nautolan from Glee Anselm, Kit Fisto can live in air or water. His head tentacles are highly sensitive olfactory organs that allow him to precisely detect subconscious pheromonal expressions of emotion. This ability allows him to take instant advantage of an opponent's uncertainty.

Jedi utility belt

Even as a senior Council member, Windu wears standard robes

Jedi tunic allows ease of movement in combat

BULTAR SWAN
Jedi Knight Bultar Swan draws in her opponents by minimizing her physical movements, striking suddenly with a flawless attack that may be highly complex, yet executed in a single blaze of motion.

Synthetic leather surcoat

Lightsaber traditionally worn at left

Power indicator

Electrum finish for Council senior only

Crystal chamber

Handgrip

As a senior member of the Jedi Council, Mace Windu built a new lightsaber for himself. Displaying the highest standards of precision, it represents Mace's mature abilities as a Jedi leader.

Jedi boots offer excellent traction

Mace Windu

A Form VII instructor, Mace Windu is one of the best living lightsaber fighters in the Jedi Order. Only high-level masters of multiple forms can achieve and control Form VII. This dangerous regimen cuts perilously close to the Sith focus on physical combat ability.

Blade projection plate

Activator

Handgrip ridges

Blade length adjust

KIT FISTO'S LIGHTSABER

Activator matrix

Blade length adjust

Radiator casing segment

BULTAR SWAN'S LIGHTSABER

JEDI WEAPONS
Every hand-built lightsaber expresses the individuality of its builder, although there are few differences in function.

PLO KOON'S LIGHTSABER

Shaak Ti

Shaak Ti fights at her best in group combat as she is biologically adapted for moving in dense crowds. She darts with ease through chaotic melees, where others struggle amidst the complexity of movements.

Hollow montrals sense space ultrasonically

Intense gaze is half-inward

Two-handed grip for control

Barriss Offee

The Padawan learner of Luminara Unduli, Barriss specializes in tandem fighting. She uses the Force to harmonize her actions perfectly with her partner, making for a pair that is more powerful than the sum of its parts.

Common lightsaber design

Mirialan tattoos

Jedi in battle must resist the temptation to use the evil power of hate and anger, even against Sith enemies.

Headdress conceals extrasensory organs sensitive to dryness

Tattoo represents dedication to a physical specialization

Luminara Unduli

Through many years of practice, Luminara has increased her joints' flexibility to easily allow extreme lightsaber moves that are impossible for ordinary humanoids.

DATA FILE

❭ Special lightsaber disciplines take advantage of non-humanoid abilities such as 360-degree vision.

❭ Jedi train constantly with their lightsabers, whether alone on long field assignments or with colleagues at the Temple.

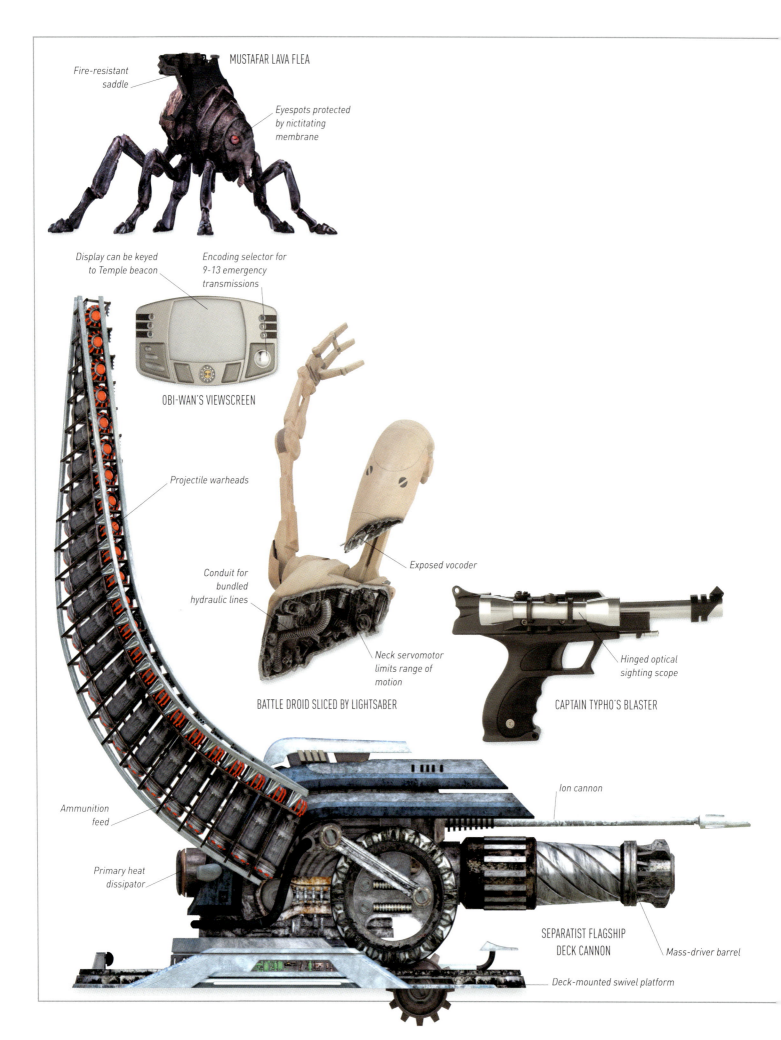

MUSTAFAR LAVA FLEA

Fire-resistant saddle

Eyespots protected by nictitating membrane

Display can be keyed to Temple beacon

Encoding selector for 9-13 emergency transmissions

OBI-WAN'S VIEWSCREEN

Projectile warheads

Conduit for bundled hydraulic lines

Exposed vocoder

Neck servomotor limits range of motion

BATTLE DROID SLICED BY LIGHTSABER

Hinged optical sighting scope

CAPTAIN TYPHO'S BLASTER

Ammunition feed

Primary heat dissipator

Ion cannon

SEPARATIST FLAGSHIP DECK CANNON

Mass-driver barrel

Deck-mounted swivel platform

EPISODE III
REVENGE OF THE SITH

STAR WARS: REVENGE OF THE SITH is at once the concluding chapter to events that have shaped the Prequel Trilogy—the era of the Republic—and a tragic prologue to the Dark Times—the 19-year period that witnesses the consolidation of power by Sith Lord Sidious and his pieced-together executioner, Darth Vader. Detailed in this chapter are the key players in the fall of the Jedi Order, the ascendancy of the dark side of the Force, and the emergence of the dreaded Empire, founded on a mad lust for power and fortified by weapons the likes of which the galaxy has never seen. Brought to life in film stills and original art are the exotic locations that serve as stages for this episode, the hardware of galactic warfare, and profiles of the many subsidiary characters caught up in this numbing climax.

Revenge of the Sith is a tale forged in chaos, informed by deceit, betrayal, heartbreak, and the death of heroes. A story almost 30 years in the making, and one that will be told and retold here, and in galaxies far, far away....

Ablative hull plates

CONFEDERACY
ESCAPE POD

Transparisteel
viewport

Jedi tunic

Utility pouch
medkit

OBI-WAN KENOBI
VERSUS ANAKIN
SKYWALKER

Tall travel
boots

Padawan
braid has
been ritually
clipped

Synthleather
surcoat

Field combat
trousers

Galactic War

FOR THREE YEARS, the Clone Wars have raged across the stars. In deep space and on a host of disparate worlds, the forces of the Republic and those of the Confederacy of Independent Systems (CIS) battle for supremacy. On one side stands a droid army led by a former Jedi named Count Dooku; on the other, an army of cloned soldiers led by the Jedi themselves, the galaxy's one-time guardians of peace. Few can explain why the conflict began, and fewer still understand what is at risk. In fact, the war is being waged by advocates of the dark side of the Force against those who call the Force their ally.

Coruscant

The varied denizens of Coruscant experienced the war from a safe distance, confident in the belief that Supreme Chancellor Palpatine could keep the fighting confined to the outer systems. But in such a conflict, no world can remain untouched. So, finally, the war stabs even at the galactic capital itself, with a daring move by the Separatist forces, led by General Grievous, to abduct the Supreme Chancellor, raising the stakes to higher than they have ever been.

Above Coruscant, Republic and Separatist warships attack each other, after Grievous's MagnaGuards and battle droids have abducted Palpatine. Anakin and Obi-Wan Kenobi speed to Palpatine's rescue.

Utapau

An Outer Rim world of vast, arid plains and immense sinkholes, Utapau is a peaceful planet with few ties to either the Republic or the CIS. But, like Coruscant, the planet cannot escape the long reach of the war, and finds itself dragged to the forefront when droid forces under General Grievous's command invade and occupy. The Pau'an and Utai populations know that the liberation of their planet is in the hands of the Jedi Knights.

Kashyyyk

For countless millennia, the skillful and resourceful Wookiees have lived in harmony with the towering wroshyr trees that dominate Kashyyyk's lush forests. But the Clone Wars bring changes even here, first with an invasion by Trandoshan slavers in league with the Separatists, then by legions of battle droids dispatched by Grievous to subjugate the entire planet.

Polarized T-visor
reduces glare

Battle-damaged
chest plastron

Cooling
backpack
turbine

Mustafar

The sulphurous skies
of Mustafar are filled
with fire and ash and its
craggy surface is slagged by
ceaseless floes of lava. This remote planet
is the last in a long list chosen by Darth Sidious
to serve as a sanctuary for the hounded members
of the Separatist Council. On hellish Mustafar,
the final acts of the Sith plot will be played
out, resulting in the deaths of enemies, the
deaths of friends—and, ultimately,
the death of love.

Kubazian skirt

Standard DC-15
blaster has a
folding stock

In service to the long-snouted aliens who oversee the
Separatists' smelting facilities on Mustafar, agile lava
fleas leap across the fiery surface.

MUSTAFARIAN

CLONE TROOPER
Symbol of the Grand
Army of the Republic,
the clone trooper has
become a ubiquitous
presence on embattled
worlds throughout the
galaxy. In the grim theater
that is the Clone War, the
trooper is also a mindless
actor in a diabolical plot to
topple the galaxy into darkness.

Anakin Skywalker

JEDI KNIGHT

AS THE CLONE TROOPER has become the emblem for the Grand Army of the Republic, Anakin Skywalker—dashing pilot and audacious Jedi Knight—has become the symbol of the Jedi Order and poster boy of the entire war effort. Praised by Supreme Chancellor Palpatine, applauded by the Senate, glorified on the HoloNet News, the "Hero With No Fear" is held by many to be the warrior-savior of the Republic. It is therefore only fitting that Anakin should rescue Palpatine from the evil clutches of General Grievous aboard the giant flagship as it attempts to flee Coruscant.

Ideal for outwitting the in-close weaponry of Grievous's flagship, *Invisible Hand*, Anakin's Jedi Interceptor slips along its turreted hull and infiltrates a docking bay.

Due to communication blunders among Republic forces, Grievous's flagship is blown in half with Palpatine aboard. Anakin and R2-D2 guide what remains of the ship to a controlled crash on Coruscant.

Electrostatic fingertips allow some feeling

Ribbing and clamps ensure tight fit

Armored shielding bulks glove and protects electromotive lines

Alloy ligaments provide pronation and supination

Electrodrivers for pistons

Glove auto-seal

ANAKIN'S GLOVE

Interface modules link prosthesis to surviving nerves

R2-D2 in astromech socket

JEDI STARFIGHTER
Anakin asked that his starfighter be painted yellow, allegedly in tribute to the Podracer he flew as a youth, but perhaps to call attention to himself in battle.

Lateral laser cannon

Cyborg Limb

Some Jedi Council members believe that when Anakin lost his right arm to Count Dooku, he lost some of his humanity. The result has been a chip on his shoulder to go with the prosthesis. In fact, Anakin has always been at ease with technology, and tinkers with his arm as he does his starfighter.

Even though Anakin is envious of Obi-Wan's place on the Jedi Council, they remain the best of friends and the most dynamic of Jedi partners, especially during the Outer Rim sieges.

Anakin believes that the political decisions should be made quickly and decisively. He is free to air his convictions to Supreme Chancellor Palpatine, who is a mentor to him in the ways of the real world.

Gauntlet worn in combat

Synthleather surcoat

Aggressive stance

Chosen One?

Torn by a desire to accomplish great things, Anakin is fearful of change. While he is generally believed to be the Chosen One alluded to in an ancient Jedi prophecy, Anakin frequently finds his hands tied, in the same way that the Senate binds the hands of Supreme Chancellor Palpatine. Nevertheless, he is determined to honor Obi-Wan, and to live up to the title the Jedi have seen fit to bestow upon him.

Utility pouch for emergency rations

Double-Agent

When Palpatine appoints Anakin to the Jedi High Council to serve as his voice, the Council counters by ordering Anakin to spy on the Supreme Chancellor. In addition, the Council withholds from Anakin the title of Master, despite his accomplishments and his mastery of the Force. Discouraged to learn that the Jedi are not above duplicity, Anakin no longer feels guilty about the fact that he has kept secrets from them.

Anakin hasn't seen Padmé—or Coruscant—in almost five months. Their forbidden marriage is yet another lie Anakin has had to maintain since the start of the Clone Wars—a secret he is reluctant to share even with Palpatine, much less with Obi-Wan.

Tunic apron

Military grade trousers

Grappling hook and line

MUSTAFAR

On Mustafar, Anakin's love for Padmé and Obi-Wan mutates to hatred when he convinces himself that his wife and his former Master have betrayed him. A Sith now, having accepted Darth Sidious as his Master and Darth Vader as his name, Anakin shows no remorse in Force-choking Padmé, and engaging Obi-Wan in a duel to the death.

UTILITY POUCH

DATA FILE

> Anakin's facial scar is a reminder of his encounter with Dooku-trained Asajj Ventress.

> Anakin was named a Jedi Knight after his actions on the planet Praesitlyn, where he almost single-handedly saved a Republic communications facility.

Durable grip-sole boots

General Kenobi

IMPERTURBABLE IN BATTLE, in deep space or planetside, General Obi-Wan Kenobi still prefers negotiation to conflict. The war, however, has given him a longer view of things. Where even his lightsaber technique once reflected an affinity for deflection, his style has since become bolder and more lethal. The cause, many say, is the influence of Anakin Skywalker, and indeed Obi-Wan has become Anakin's champion to those on the Council who dread the power of the Chosen One. As a result of his military successes in the Outer Rim, General Kenobi has been granted the title "Master," and named to the Council. Even so, he feels that his education in the Force is just beginning.

Spacious, pressurized cockpit module

R4-P17 received a full body at the start of the war

Jedi/Bendu-inspired emblem, symbol of the Republic

JEDI INTERCEPTOR
Obi-Wan hates piloting, and has scant regard for astromech or other droids. Yet, he remains Anakin's steadfast wingmate in battle, trusting Anakin to pull them through tricky situations. Just as Anakin has learned patience from Obi-Wan, Obi-Wan has been spurred on to take risks.

Return Bout

Wingtip to wingtip flying is only one aspect of Obi-Wan and Anakin's friendship and mutual trust. They attack Count Dooku in concert aboard the Separatist command cruiser, lulling him into a false sense of confidence by using standard lightsaber tactics, only to shift to advanced forms, forcing a confused Dooku to retreat.

Despite his failure to take Dooku into captivity, Obi-Wan is held in great esteem by the members of the Jedi Council, who conclude that Obi-Wan is the only person skilled enough to capture the elusive and dangerous General Grievous on Utapau.

Rangefinder lock

Cushioned eyecup

JEDI MACROBINOCULARS

Projection platform

Duranium cinch-locks

SEPARATIST BINDERS

Can be uncoupled by the Force

HOLOPROJECTOR   Casing ring

Leaving Anakin to face the hordes of media correspondents that flock to the flagship's crash site, Obi-Wan confers with Yoda regarding their fears that the Sith have been controlling the war from the beginning, and that Darth Sidious himself may be someone close to the Supreme Chancellor.

Powerful tail, 10 meters (33 feet) long

Spines for defense

Crest present in both male and female

Five-clawed feet provide excellent purchase

Unusually grave expression

Robe is Obi-Wan's sixth since start of war

BOGA

On Utapau, Obi-Wan selects a varactyl that he senses has a constant commitment to obedience and care for her rider. Boga clambers to the tenth level of Pau City with a swiftness that surprises even Obi-Wan, only to fall later in a hail of blaster fire unleashed by turncoat Clone Troopers.

Compressed-air tank

REBREATHER

The A99 Aquata Breather Obi-Wan had used on Naboo 13 years earlier serves him all the more on Utapau.

Obi-Wan knows that Anakin pines for Senator Padmé Amidala. Throughout the war, Obi-Wan has watched Anakin grow more powerful, willful, and conflicted.

Jedi Tradition

Honoring the wishes of his former Master, Qui-Gon Jinn, Obi-Wan has made Anakin his life's focus, and has instilled in Anakin his belief that the dark side can be defeated and the Force brought back into balance. Yet Obi-Wan worries about Anakin's refusal to surrender the past, especially his fixation with his mother's death.

Security recordings are stored in the Jedi Temple data room

Obi-Wan's worst fears for Anakin are realized when a Jedi Temple security recording proves that Anakin has turned to the dark side, pledged himself to the Sith, and has been responsible for the murder of many Jedi Knights and younglings.

Fabric looks heavier than it is

Traditional blue blade

DATA FILE

› Shortly before the end of the war, Obi-Wan and Anakin attempt but fail to capture Dooku's dark-side apprentice, Asajj Ventress, who remains at large.

› Partnered with Obi-Wan during most of the war, R4-P17 is destroyed by buzz droids during the Battle of Coruscant.

Jedi Knight

OBI-WAN SHARES Anakin's eagerness to confront Count Dooku and repay him in kind for the defeat they suffered on Geonosis. As a Jedi, though, Obi-Wan refuses to let his emotions cloud his better judgment, and fixes his attention on Supreme Chancellor Palpatine. "Rescue not mayhem," he counsels Anakin. Rendered unconscious during the duel, Obi-Wan does not witness the Count's death. However, he persuades himself that his willful former Padawan was forced to act in self-defense and has not skirted close to what the Jedi consider the dark side of the Force. Obi-Wan suspects that Palpatine has convinced Anakin that anything which is possible must be allowed.

Niman stance, with blade cocked high

Utility belt houses pouches for rebreather, comlink, and liquid-cable launcher

The fight between Obi-Wan and Anakin leads to the collapse of Mustafar's shields

Obi-Wan and Anakin have been partnered for so long that they can all but read each other's minds and predict what each other will do.

Swordmaster

Though a master of the Jedi lightsaber style known as Ataru, in which deflection is prized above aggression, Obi-Wan's true style is Soresu, which encourages a practitioner to place himself at the eye of the storm. Soresu is well served by Obi-Wan's innate capacity for patience and perception, but the key to mastery is audacity, a talent he has learned from Anakin.

In Anakin's flair for the dramatic and his disregard for the rules, Obi-Wan finds troubling echoes of Qui-Gon Jinn. Although Obi-Wan's student, Anakin helped mold his Master into the great Jedi Qui-Gon always thought Obi-Wan might be. This is ironic when Kenobi is forced to fight his own apprentice whom Qui-Gon ordered to be trained in the Jedi arts.

Power cell reserve cap

Ridged handgrip

OBI-WAN'S LIGHTSABER
Though it often slips from his grip, Obi-Wan's lightsaber will remain in his possession for his 19 years of self-exile on Tatooine, watching over young Luke Skywalker.

DATA FILE

› Obi-Wan is not without his secrets, including a relationship with Jedi Siri Tachi, who died saving Padmé.

› Obi-Wan is mystified by Anakin's attachment to R2-D2, and even more by the astromech's apparent attachment to Anakin.

Leading foot is firmly planted

Dooku—Sith Apprentice

THE TITLE OF COUNT has no real meaning to Dooku, the former Jedi. It is simply the name of the political leader of the Confederacy of Independent Systems, which itself is nothing more than a fabrication, conceived by Darth Sidious as part of his plan to topple the Jedi Order and reinstate the Sith. For more than a decade now, "Dooku" has thought of himself as Darth Tyranus, apprentice to Sidious and destined to sit at his left hand as joint master of the galaxy.

Signature look of superiority

Costly hand-woven tunic was made on Vjun

A shackled Palpatine watches Dooku and Anakin duel aboard the Separatist flagship. In fact, the abduction is an elaborate ruse, engineered to ensnare Anakin and test him to determine whether he can be turned to the dark side.

Dooku's Jedi and Sith pasts meet as Anakin scissors two lightsabers at his neck. Too late, Dooku realizes Anakin is more powerful than he could have imagined.

Blade-emitter guard

Magnetic adhesion plate

DOOKU'S LIGHTSABER

Easily Replaceable

Sidious had promised to intervene in the duel, in the unlikely event that Anakin gained the upper hand. But intervention, too, was never part of the real plan. Blinded by pride, Dooku has failed to grasp that, like Darth Maul before him, he is little more than a placeholder for the apprentice Sidious has sought from the beginning: Skywalker himself.

Dress boots of rare rancor leather

DATA FILE

> Dooku's turn to the dark side began with the murder of Jedi Master Sifo-Dyas, his former friend and confidant in the Order. Assuming control of the plans Sifo-Dyas had set in motion to create a clone army for the Republic, Dooku saw to it that all mention of the planet Kamino was erased from Jedi Archives.

Separatist Ground Forces

THE SUPPLIERS OF SEPARATIST war machines have a long history of manufacturing droids to suit a wide range of uses and environments. The fearsome appearance of the military droids owes much to the fact that the insectoid species involved in the design phase use themselves as models. Faced with glowing photoreceptors that resemble eyes, stabilizers that mimic claws, and laser cannons that might be appendages, the soldiers of the Republic's non-clone ground forces almost forget that they are battling droids, and not living creatures.

BATTLE DROIDS
Mainstay of the Separatist infantry, battle droids are churned out on Techno Union foundry worlds. They answer to central computers, but words confuse them as much as bolts and lightsabers destroy them.

DROIDEKAS
One of the most feared armaments of the Separatist's surface arsenal, the droideka, or destroyer droid, is a self-shielded annihilator, able to deliver devastating packets of raw firepower. Droidekas help capture Obi-Wan and Anakin during their flight from the General's Quarters on Grievous's flagship, with a rescued Palpatine.

Pincer heat exhaust

Armorplast shielding

Reinforced alloy lifting rods

Communication/ sensor stalks

Sensor bulb

Blast shielding safeguards droid brain

Secondary photoreceptor

Targetting rangefinder

Twin blasters

Pressurized bolt

Prongs extend for added purchase

Pincers powered by proprietary motors

Lateral stabilizer

Crab Droid

Known to clone troopers as "The Muckracker," the crab droid is deployed on marshy worlds, such as Utapau. Heavily armored and ranging from surveillance drones that are one meter (three feet) tall to trailblazers that are six meters (twenty feet) tall, the droid can scuttle through muck to create tracks for infantry. Its front pincers also serve as vacuums, slurping up and spewing out lake-bed mud.

Duranium stabilizer can plunge into bedrock

HOMING SPIDER DROID
The Commerce Guild's contribution to the ground war is the homing spider droid. It is an all-terrain weapon capable of precise targeting and sustained beam fire from its laser cannons. With surface-to-air and surface-to-surface abilities, it is a danger to Republic walkers and gunships.

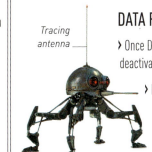

Tracing antenna

DATA FILE

› Once Darth Sidious announces that the war has ended, deactivation orders are sent to battle droids.

› Most Separatist war machines are deactivated at the end of the Clone Wars, but the dwarf spider droids are used by the Empire to enforce the submission of once-Separatist strongholds.

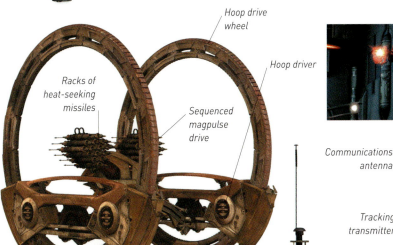

Hoop drive wheel

Racks of heat-seeking missiles

Hoop driver

Sequenced magpulse drive

HAILFIRE DROID
Once used by the InterGalactic Banking Clan for debt collection, the missile platform is a central component of the Separatists' rapid-deployment force. Retired from the battlefield due to its limited supply of 30 warheads, the swift, self-aware hailfire was later partnered with an air-mobile refresh droid, and regained its reputation for being the scourge of slow-moving targets.

Archduke Poggle the Lesser's super battle droid resembles a carapaced beetle, reared up on hind legs. Little more than an infantry droid in a durable shell, the improved model is single-minded about the task of killing.

NR-N99 Tank Droid

Once employed to persuade corporations of the wisdom of being acquired by the Corporate Alliance, the tank droid quickly became a staple in the Clone Wars, and was deployed to the Separatists' advantage on Geonosis, Kashyyyk, Cato Neimoidia, and many other worlds.
An amphibious war machine, the tank can race across flat ground or shallow lakes. The circular-bodied automatons utilized early in the war were replaced by droid-piloted models, featuring superior firepower and targeting. Its treads provide amazing traction, and its side platforms are running boards for infantry droids.

Communications antenna

Tracking transmitter

Stereoscopic sensor

Drive axis hub

Primary drive tread

Modular ion cannon

Heat exchangers

Weapons outrigger

Pontoon tread

Laser cannon

R2-D2
VERSATILE OPERATOR

A QUIRKY, ONE-IN-A-MILLION DROID, R2-D2 has come a long way since serving as aboard Queen Amidala's royal starship. Time and again, the astromech has exceeded his programming, not only in the socket of a Jedi starfighter but on scores of occasions on as many worlds. He seems to delight in belittling his officious protocol counterparts, and is so perfectly attuned to Anakin's fighting spirit he may as well have been custom-built for him. Stubborn, courageous, and loyal, R2-D2 has displayed remarkable determination to succeed, despite the odds.

As battle-scarred as any droid of the Republic fleet, R2-D2 provides Anakin's Jedi Interceptor with updates on ship's status, navigation, and battle assessment. The droid, with a mind of his own, always carries out his tasks, yet considers starfighter duty a boring day job.

ARTFUL DODGER
As cunning as an intelligence operative, R2-D2 can blend in with his surroundings. Thus, he is often overlooked when super battle droids search for enemies, or starship captains memory-wipe their droids. Many underestimate R2-D2's retention powers, which will one day amaze the galaxy.

Multi-Taskmaster

Originally, only R2-D2's colors distinguished him from other astromechs. Now, courtesy of his new owner, he hosts a variety of attachments and modifications. Anakin has tweaked the droid's processor and memory matrices, and improved his interchangeable component design by upgrading his tool kit. As a result, R2-D2 can render rapid analyses of computer and starfighter weapons systems.

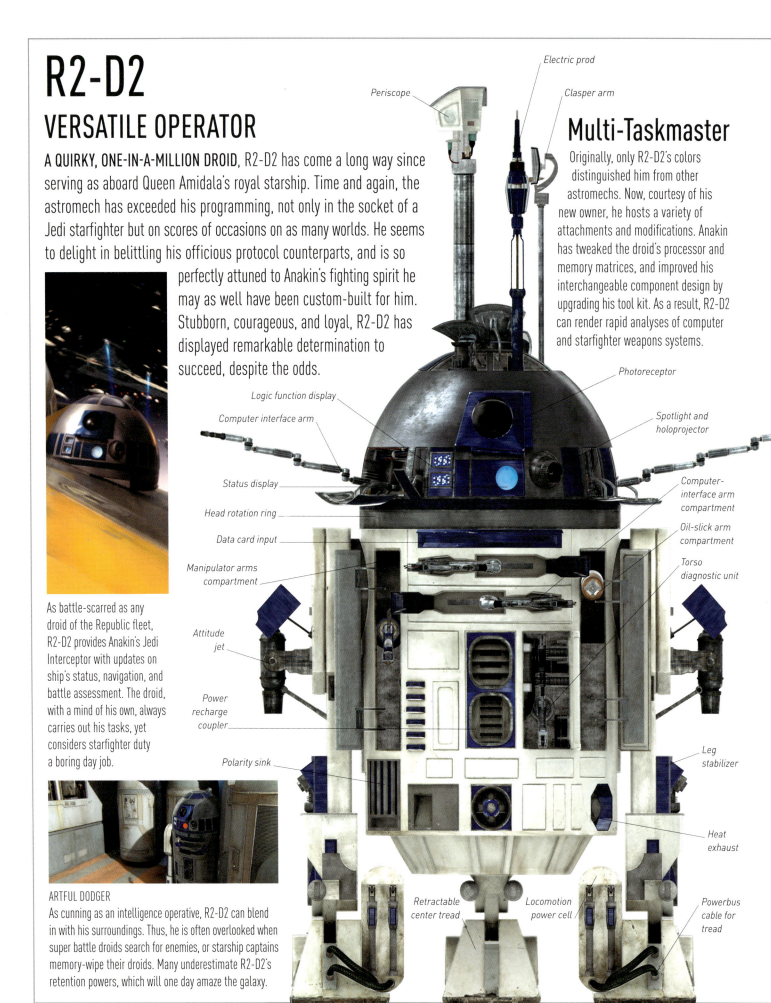

Electric prod

Periscope

Clasper arm

Photoreceptor

Logic function display

Computer interface arm

Spotlight and holoprojector

Status display

Computer-interface arm compartment

Head rotation ring

Oil-slick arm compartment

Data card input

Torso diagnostic unit

Manipulator arms compartment

Attitude jet

Power recharge coupler

Leg stabilizer

Polarity sink

Heat exhaust

Retractable center tread

Locomotion power cell

Powerbus cable for tread

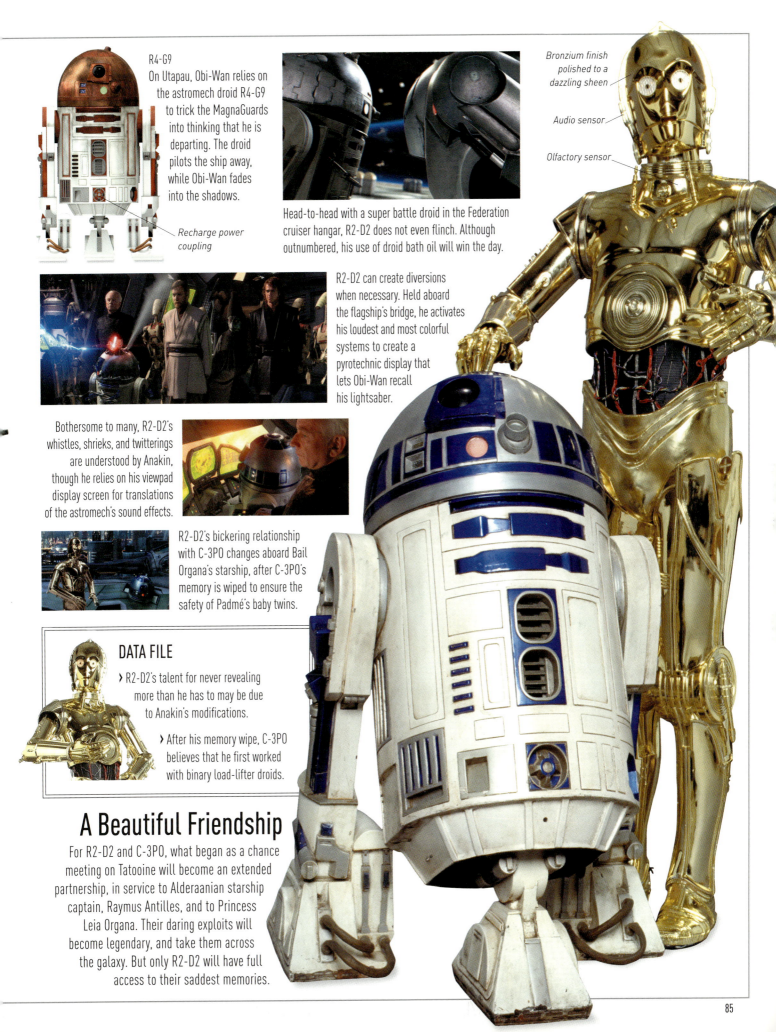

R4-G9
On Utapau, Obi-Wan relies on the astromech droid R4-G9 to trick the MagnaGuards into thinking that he is departing. The droid pilots the ship away, while Obi-Wan fades into the shadows.

Recharge power coupling

Bronzium finish polished to a dazzling sheen

Audio sensor

Olfactory sensor

Head-to-head with a super battle droid in the Federation cruiser hangar, R2-D2 does not even flinch. Although outnumbered, his use of droid bath oil will win the day.

R2-D2 can create diversions when necessary. Held aboard the flagship's bridge, he activates his loudest and most colorful systems to create a pyrotechnic display that lets Obi-Wan recall his lightsaber.

Bothersome to many, R2-D2's whistles, shrieks, and twitterings are understood by Anakin, though he relies on his viewpad display screen for translations of the astromech's sound effects.

R2-D2's bickering relationship with C-3PO changes aboard Bail Organa's starship, after C-3PO's memory is wiped to ensure the safety of Padmé's baby twins.

DATA FILE
> R2-D2's talent for never revealing more than he has to may be due to Anakin's modifications.

> After his memory wipe, C-3PO believes that he first worked with binary load-lifter droids.

A Beautiful Friendship

For R2-D2 and C-3PO, what began as a chance meeting on Tatooine will become an extended partnership, in service to Alderaanian starship captain, Raymus Antilles, and to Princess Leia Organa. Their daring exploits will become legendary, and take them across the galaxy. But only R2-D2 will have full access to their saddest memories.

Supreme Chancellor Palpatine

UNFLINCHING IN HIS ASSERTION that a Republic divided against itself cannot stand, Palpatine has devoted almost half of his unprecedented 13 years in office to vanquishing the Separatist threat. Gracious and unassuming before the outbreak of the Clone Wars, he has since become Democracy's fierce champion, sacrificing his private life to assume the burden of leading the Republic to victory, the Jedi at his right hand, the Grand Army of the Republic at his left. Determined to preserve the Constitution at all costs, he is quick to maintain that he will gladly relinquish the extraordinary powers the Senate has seen fit to cede him, once the Separatists have been eliminated.

Hair is always immaculately arranged

Expression promises safety, security, justice, and peace

Senatorial collar

Cummerbund of high office

The General's Quarters aboard *Invisible Hand* bear an eerie similarity to Palpatine's chambers in the Senate Office Building. When Anakin and Obi-Wan arrive, Count Dooku is there to welcome them. Neither Jedi realizes that Dooku and Palpatine are not enemies to each other, but confederates.

Beneath the Mask

To some, Palpatine's guileless smile belies the visage of a shadowy, self-serving politician. Isolated by a covey of advisors, he is frequently at odds with the Jedi Council regarding the course of the war. Adept at manipulating public opinion, he buoys the Republic with carefully controlled HoloNet reports. Bent on executing a hidden agenda, he uses the war to place himself in a position where his word is law.

Aboard Grievous's devastated flagship, Palpatine shows remarkable strength and dexterity by negotiating a precarious elevator shaft and corridors turned topsy-turvy by ruined gravity projectors.

DATA FILE

> Records of Palpatine's ancestry, immediate family members, and upbringing on Naboo have mysteriously vanished.

> Captain Panaka, former Head of Security for Queen Amidala, gave Palpatine information regarding Anakin and Padmé's secret marriage.

Ancient demagogue, Sistros

Lethorns have thickened over the years

Speaker's staff

Chagrian cowl

Umbarans conceal their emotions

Palpatine has counseled Anakin in worldly matters, and listened to his dark confessions regarding his anger, his infatuation with Padmé, his frustrations with the Jedi Council, and even his slaughter of a tribe of Sand People on Tatooine. Their almost familial relationship is a cause of great concern to the Council.

Secret Fraternity

Senate Speaker, Mas Amedda, and Aide to the Chancellor, Sly Moore, are two among a select few who understand that Palpatine is more than he appears and that the Chancellor's look of practiced humility belies that of a cunning manipulator of political power. Palpatine's duplicity could ultimately cost them their positions—and their lives.

SLY MOORE

Force pike

Contents unknown

SITH CHALICE

Palpatine declares the Republic an Empire and himself Emperor following the defeat of the Jedi responsible for the hideous change in his appearance.

IMPERIAL GUARD
With the creation of the Empire, the Red Guard becomes the Imperial Guard. Palpatine picked its members from non-clone military units.

Shadowcloak of the Ghost Nebula

MAS AMEDDA

Though his face is irreparably damaged, Palpatine's integrity and resolve are intact and he becomes authority personified. Safety, Security, Justice, and Peace are the bywords of the New Order.

General Grievous

UNKNOWN TO THE JEDI until he battled them on the Separatist foundry world of Hypori, General Grievous was actually present at the Battle of Geonosis. The carnage for which he was responsible, however, was confined to the catacombs that undermined Archduke Poggle the Lesser's Stalgasin hive complex. Named Supreme Commander of the Droid Armies in the wake of Geonosis, Grievous brought new levels of butchery to the war, laying waste to entire worlds and populations, and leaving trails of blood wherever he ventured in the Outer or Mid Rims. Although he is a cyborg, Grievous does not consider himself a droid, and reacts savagely to any such inference—as his victims would attest.

The blade of Jedi Master Puroth

Abetted by Darths Sidious and Tyranus, Grievous carried out the long-planned abduction of Palpatine from the Chancellor's bunker on Coruscant. Unaware that he is serving both Sidious and Palpatine, Grievous does not understand why he cannot assassinate Palpatine.

DATA FILE

> Grievous can dislocate his shoulders and split his two arms into four.

> The General is secretly humiliated at having been resurrected as a cyborg.

Duranium head

Phrik alloy

Impact-driven release

Retracted claws

High output magazine

BLASTECH CUSTOM DT-57 "ANNIHILATOR"

Weapons of War

The uniwheel chariot Grievous pilots on Utapau is outfitted with a variety of weapons, including a powerful blaster, an energy staff of the sort wielded by his elite MagnaGuards, and a grappling hook, similar to the one he used at Coruscant to haul himself to freedom along the hull of his crippled flagship.

Power-assisted shaft

GRAPPLING HOOK

Palpatine lures Obi-Wan to Separatist-occupied Utapau. With Kenobi thus occupied, Anakin has no one to guide him and is more likely to listen to the dark side.

Weapons pack

Electromagnetic pulse generator

ENERGY STAFF

Transparisteel viewports

Hyperspace engine

Landing gear

TOP VIEW

FIGHTER
Escaping from Utapau, Obi-Wan learns that Grievous's starfighter is hyperspace-capable. After the clone trooper attack, he transmits a 9-13 Jedi emergency code over the HoloNet repeater.

Grievous's hatred of the Jedi goes back to his former life as a Kaleesh warlord. Grievous captured his first lightsaber from a Jedi he defeated, and his collection has expanded ever since.

Original mask carved from Mumuu skull

Sallow reptilian eyes

Engraved lines simulate original mask's karabba-blood war paint

Ultrasonic vocabulator

Electro-driven arms can split in half

Reinforced knee plates

Leg drivers house crystal circuitry

Upgraded LX-44 legs

Powerful magnetized talons

Cape contains sheath pockets for lightsabers

Alien Warlord

Grievous's reputation as a warlord was forged during a brutal war between the Kaleesh and the Huk species. On the brink of death following a shuttle crash, Grievous was rebuilt. Neither Force-sensitive nor a Sith, the cyborg general was trained in lightsaber combat by Darth Tyranus, and is more than a match for most Jedi.

MagnaGuards

STRIDING DEFIANTLY across the surface-ravaged Huk worlds, Kaleesh warlord General Grievous was always accompanied by an elite group of warriors and bodyguards. Rebuilt as Supreme Commander of the Separatist army, he has to content himself with the Trade Federation's battle droids, which answer to a central control computer and are incapable of learning from their mistakes. Apprised of Grievous's disdain for these droids, Darth Tyranus authorizes Holowan Mechanicals to manufacture the Prototype Self-Motivating Heuristically Programmed Combat Droid, or IG-series 100 MagnaGuard, built to Grievous's specifications and trained by him.

The MagnaGuards score a victory on *Invisible Hand*, taking Anakin, Obi-Wan, and Supreme Chancellor Palpatine into custody after the trio are trapped in a ray-shielded stretch of corridor. But General Grievous's gloating is short-lived, however, after a diversionary move by R2-D2 sends the bridge into chaos.

When the smoke clears, the MagnaGuards are in pieces. The remainder of Grievous's elite will suffer a similar fate on Utapau, in a warm-up round for Obi-Wan's match with the cyborg commander.

Model Guards

Holowan Mechanicals made several MagnaGuard models, distinguished by color: black, alabaster, blue, and the rare gray. Each two-meter (6.5-ft) tall droid specializes in a form of combat, and is equipped with an electrostaff or dedicated weapons, from grenades to rocket launchers. Headclothes pay tribute to those worn by Grievous's original elite.

Electrostaffs

Constructed of costly phrik alloy and equipped with electromagnetic pulse-generating tips, the MagnaGuards electrostaffs are resistant to lightsaber strikes. While certain types of staff are capable of neutralizing ray shields, the standard staff serves primarily as a melee weapon, meting out fatal blunt-force injuries in the hands of its wielders.

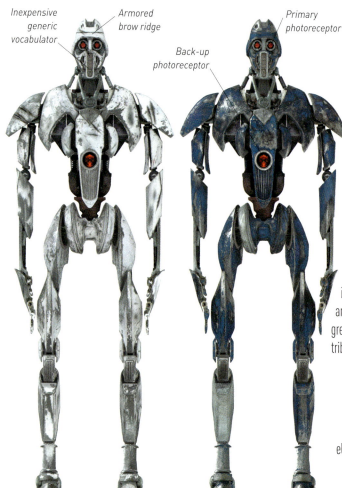

Inexpensive generic vocabulator

Armored brow ridge

Primary photoreceptor

Back-up photoreceptor

Discharge capacitor

Power cycling coil

Power cell

EMP field generator

Focusing rods

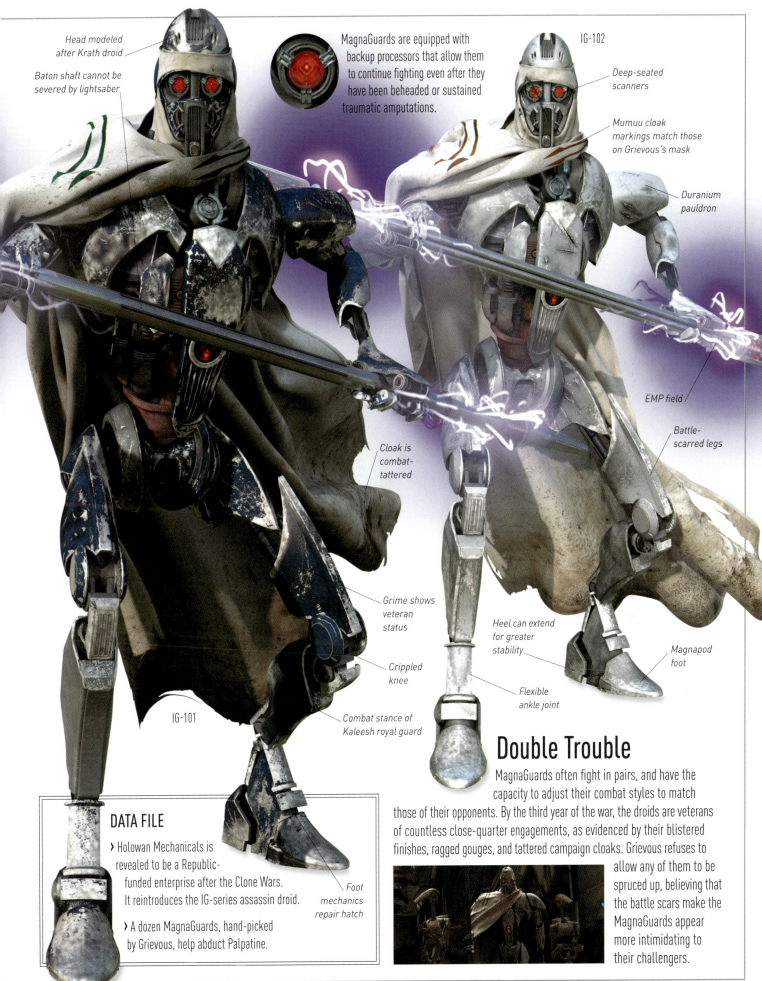

Head modeled after Krath droid

Baton shaft cannot be severed by lightsaber

MagnaGuards are equipped with backup processors that allow them to continue fighting even after they have been beheaded or sustained traumatic amputations.

IG-102

Deep-seated scanners

Mumuu cloak markings match those on Grievous's mask

Duranium pauldron

EMP field

Battle-scarred legs

Cloak is combat-tattered

Grime shows veteran status

Crippled knee

Combat stance of Kaleesh royal guard

Heel can extend for greater stability

Flexible ankle joint

Magnapod foot

IG-101

DATA FILE

› Holowan Mechanicals is revealed to be a Republic-funded enterprise after the Clone Wars. It reintroduces the IG-series assassin droid.

› A dozen MagnaGuards, hand-picked by Grievous, help abduct Palpatine.

Foot mechanics repair hatch

Double Trouble

MagnaGuards often fight in pairs, and have the capacity to adjust their combat styles to match those of their opponents. By the third year of the war, the droids are veterans of countless close-quarter engagements, as evidenced by their blistered finishes, ragged gouges, and tattered campaign cloaks. Grievous refuses to allow any of them to be spruced up, believing that the battle scars make the MagnaGuards appear more intimidating to their challengers.

Padmé—Tragic Heroine

TIME AND AGAIN Padmé has found herself at the center of galactic events. Her illegal presence on Geonosis to effect the rescue of Obi-Wan Kenobi is seen by some as the spark that ignited the Clone Wars. Padmé has earned a reputation for boldness, but now she is torn by choices she has made in her private life, and she sometimes dreams of retiring into seclusion on Naboo. However, her activist side is not easily suppressed.

Elaborate coiffure originated on Naboo

Heirloom suspensas

Rich cape enfolds Padmé completely

In the three years since their secret marriage on Naboo, Padmé and Anakin have found refuge in each other's embrace. But their trysts have been brief and clandestine. They haven't met in five months when Palpatine's abduction returns Anakin to Coruscant.

Anti-tracking device *Tractor field seats* *Secret compartment for blaster* *Souped-up engine*

Aerodynamic yet classic styling

CLASSIC SPEEDER
Padmé's classic-style speeder whisks her to and from the landing platform where her starship is berthed. Anakin has modified the speeder's engine.

Senator

Padmé's voice in the Senate is still as powerful as it was before the start of the war. While Anakin commands legions of clone troopers in the Outer Rim, Padmé and other members of the Loyalist Committee attempt to find peaceful resolution to the ongoing conflict. Yet her critics say that she has turned a blind eye to the increasingly oppressive climate on Coruscant, to the loss of rights guaranteed by the Constitution, and to the growing power of Palpatine.

DATA FILE

❯ Handmaidens Moteé and Ellé were chosen because they resemble Padmé. They know of her marriage to Anakin, and often facilitate the couple's meetings by serving as decoys.

❯ After the massacre at the Jedi Temple, the official explanation is that Padmé and many Senators had been killed by the Jedi.

Ensconced in Naboo's platform in the Senate Rotunda, Padmé witnesses the death of democracy, as Palpatine proclaims the Republic an Empire, and himself Emperor for life. The ovation he receives shows that anyone can fall victim to the machinations of an evil leader.

THE BEST OF TIMES

With its private landing platform, lofty veranda, and several entrances, Padmé's penthouse in the arch-topped summit of the Senate Apartment Complex is near perfect for rendezvous with Anakin. By Senatorial standards, the penthouse is modest in size and decor, though most Coruscanti would consider it to be flagrantly opulent.

Preoccupied expression

Harness eases back pain

Remote control receiver

Globe creates seemingly sourceless light

WISH GLOBE

Ancient moon goddess pose

ILLUMINATOR

Padmé has adorned her rooms with items from her Lake District residence.

SHIRAYA STATUE

Double Life

Like Anakin and Palpatine, Padmé is adept at hiding her true nature. But she is unable to completely conceal the facts of her pregnancy: the fullness of her figure and her frequent distraction. Senatorial scandals are nothing new, but Padmé's secret could destroy Anakin's life as a public hero, and forever foil his hopes of being named to the Jedi Council.

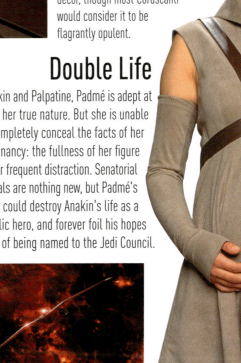

MUSTAFAR
Refusing to believe Obi-Wan when he says that Anakin has been turned to the dark side, Padmé races to Mustafar in her starship.

Gravely injured by Anakin's Force choke, Padmé is brought to a nearby medical facility on Polis Massa. Dying, despite the care she is given, she tells Obi-Wan that she still feels there is good in Anakin.

QUEEN APAILANA

Cerlin capelet

Chersilk mourning robe

Boots contain cushioned inserts

RUWEE   SOLA   JOBAL

Naboo Funeral

Padmé's parents Ruwee and Jobal, sister Sola, and Queen Apailana, are told that Padmé was killed by the Jedi on Coruscant. No mention is made of Padmé's pregnancy or where R2-D2 and C-3PO are. An investigation into who fathered the children would go against Naboo tradition.

The Senate
FAILING DEMOCRACY

WHERE GREED AND CORRUPTION defined the pre-war Senate, dereliction of duty and indolence have been the bywords since. Reasoned discourse and spirited debate are now viewed as archaic practices, impediments to the "efficient streamlining of the bureaucratic process." In the climate of fear spawned by the war, most Senators find it easier—some say safer—to place their personal convictions on hold, and to ratify any piece of legislation that cedes greater power to Supreme Chancellor Palpatine or to any of the committees responsible for overseeing the war effort. Typically, the Senate is so busy modifying the Republic Constitution that it has completely abandoned its role as a balancing arm of the government.

Republic Senate

Executive Annex Dome

SENATE BUILDING
Rising from the center of the Legislative District, the Senate comes under attack by vulture fighters and droid gunships during General Grievous's sudden raid on Coruscant. While the building emerges unscathed, nearby edifices, landing platforms, and plazas suffer major damage. In the Nicandra Counterrevolutionary Signalmen's Memorial Building alone, fatalities number in the thousands.

Sern Prime topknot

High-status beard

Senatorial gown

FANG ZAR

Fashionable translator

Molf-tasseled overcloak

Kuati turban

Formal shoulder sash

GIDDEAN DANU

Hairstyle is a plea for peace

Visdic body wrappings

MALÉ-DEE

Giddean Danu and Malé-Dee are among a group of Senators opposing Palpatine. They believe that he may respond if he is told that there are other disaffected Senators.

Noble Politicians
Palpatine and his parties of aides and red-robed guards have not cowed all the Senators. A loyal group has signed "The Petition of the Two Thousand," which states in no uncertain terms that the time has come for the Supreme Chancellor to yield some of the emergency powers that were granted him. It also demands that he open cease-fire negotiations with representatives of the Confederacy of Independent Systems.

TERR TANEEL   CHI EEKWAY

SPY CAM

Coruscanti have demonstrated a great willingness to surrender personal freedoms in the name of safety. Even severe security measures are now accepted without question. Inside the Senate, new procedures allow for eavesdropping by hovercams.

Control antenna

Telephoto lens

Privacy screens can no longer be activated in the Senate Rotunda. Many delegates are therefore afraid to whisper their reactions, let alone speak their minds. Hovercams slink about, relaying recordings to security chief Armand Isard.

Sarrish Defense Force tunic

Calamarian collar gives moisture

Beak can crack shellfish

VEEDAAZ AWMETTH

MEENA TILLS

GUME SAAM

Large, flat teeth for methodical chewing

Costly Andalian cloak

Formal Senate robes

Shimmersilk mantle

ASK AAK

SOLIPO YEB

SWEITT CONCORKILL

Heads of State

Even before the abrupt end to the Clone Wars, many Senators representing Outer Rim worlds avoided Coruscant. They feared retribution for having forged trade agreements with species identified with the Separatist movement. By contrast, those Senators who were shrewd enough to remain on Coruscant and side with Palpatine found themselves rewarded in the post-war years.

Mon Mothma

Unknown to Palpatine, the two Senators most responsible for drawing up the Petition of the Two Thousand are Bail Organa, representing the Core world Alderaan, and Mon Mothma, daughter of a former governor of Chandrila. Politically savvy but very headstrong, Mon Mothma encourages Bail to draw outspoken Padmé Amidala into their confidence, convinced that Padmé's well-known loyalty to Palpatine can work to the petitioners' advantage.

Antique Chandrilan headpiece

Serene expression

Hanna pendant

DATA FILE

> Until the election of Princess Leia Organa to the Imperial Senate, Mon Mothma is the youngest Senator ever to hold office.

> Mon Mothma, Bail Organa, and his adopted daughter, Leia, will all play pivotal roles in the formation of the Rebel Alliance.

Order 66

DESPITE THEIR INTUITIVE POWERS, the Jedi were unaware that the cloned soldiers of the Grand Army had been trained to obey, without question, numerous emergency protocols that could be activated by Supreme Chancellor Palpatine. After Palpatine was almost arrested by the Jedi Coucil on Coruscant, he initiated Order 66—a secret directive to assassinate Jedi throughout the galaxy. Upon receiving Order 66, clone commanders instantly identified the Jedi as traitors to the Republic and proceeded to murder them.

Jedi Aayla Secura is ambushed by her own troops on Felucia.

Felucia

On numerous worlds, clone troopers utilize indigenous creatures as mounts and beasts of burden, such as the large ground beetles of Felucia. It was partially due to their care for such creatures that some Jedi assume that clones possess sensitivity that could be likened to compassion. Order 66 reveals that though the clones could behave as such, their ultimate loyalty is to Palpatine.

A Felucian ground beetle, also known as a gelagrub

Ocellus detects changes in light intensity

Gelegrubs eat constantly to maintain their natural sunscreen

Prolegs offer steady locomotion

4 meters

Cato Neimoidia

One of the wealthiest worlds in the galaxy, Cato Neimoidia is the primary base for Trade Federation forces allied with the Confederacy of Independent Systems. Jedi Master Plo Koon helps to secure the planet during the Clone Wars.

Palpatine contacts Captain Jag who served under Jedi Master Plo Koon on assignment at Cato Neimoidia. Receiving the secret directive in the cockpit of his ARC-170, Jag immediately orders his squadron to shoot down the Jedi.

Jedi Master Plo Koon is piloting his customized Delta-7 Jedi starfighter when his wingmen attack on Cato Neimoidia.

After his wingmen attack, Plo Koon's damaged starfighter spins out of control before crashing into the Neimoidian cityscape.

Shielded backpack

Breath warmer cover made of synthmesh

Freeze-proof alloy

Semi-translucent skin can metabolize UV-filtering chemicals from Felucia's native plant life

Mygeeto

Stronghold of the InterGalactic Banking Clan, Mygeeto is a frigid world covered by crystallized glaciers. Palpatine dispatches a group of Coruscant-trained members of the 501st Legion to supplement the snow-armor clad Galactic Marines on Mygeeto.

After Clone Commander Bacara receives Order 66 on Mygeeto, he directs his Galactic Marines to open fire on Jedi Master Ki-Adi-Mundi. Because of their deep-core learning programs, the clones neither hesitate nor feel remorse for assassinating their leader.

DATA FILE

› Order 66 triggered the deaths of thousands of Jedi throughout the galaxy, an event that came to be known as the Jedi Purge. Among the casualties were Jedi Master Stass Allie, killed by her wingmen on recaptured Saleucami.

Cervical rib

Tail bone

Sand creature claw

TATOOINE SAND
CREATURE BONES

Multi-function
tool sheath

Neural
spine

Posterior
zygapophosis

SAND CREATURE
NECK VERTEBRA

Magnetic
insulator

LUKE SKYWALKER'S
BELT POUCH

Chime
mount

Screamer gong

Tryna
chime

Plastoid
composite
alloy

O'Tawa cymbals

DEATH STAR TROOPER'S
HELMET

Communications
antenna

Intercomlink

Resonator

Gong
stand

Centressar
strings

Flash
shield

DEATH STAR GUNNER'S HELMET

Seilith
music
charms

DRUMHELLER
HARP

Blade length
adjust

Activator
assembly

Harp
base

Emitter
shroud

DARTH VADER'S LIGHTSABER

EPISODES IV-VI
CLASSIC TRILOGY

EPISODE IV: A NEW HOPE heralds a new generation of characters that have grown up under Emperor Palpatine's iron fist. Luke Skywalker is an unlikely hero, having never left his sleepy desert home-planet of Tatooine. Upon receiving a distress call from the beautiful Princess Leia he enlists the aid of Obi-Wan Kenobi, Han Solo, and Chewbacca to rescue her from the forces of the Empire. As the adventure unfolds so do the mysteries of Luke's past. He must face up to his destiny to be a Jedi Knight, just as his father was before him.

In Episode V: *The Empire Strikes Back*, the battle to restore the Republic continues. With the Rebels' success in destroying the Death Star still fresh, the Emperor is keen to exact revenge. Using his henchman, Darth Vader, the battle for power continues unabated even when both Vader and Luke Skywalker learn the truth of their relationship.

Episode VI: *Return of the Jedi* sees Luke struggle with his internal emotions. By learning to control his anger and hate, he masters the Force and begins to control his own destiny as well as that of the galaxy....

THE EMPEROR'S CANE

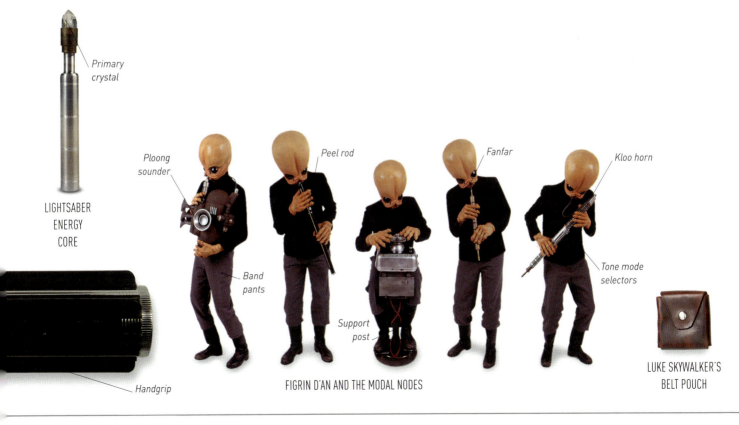

Primary crystal

LIGHTSABER ENERGY CORE

Handgrip

Ploong sounder

Peel rod

Fanfar

Kloo horn

Band pants

Support post

Tone mode selectors

FIGRIN D'AN AND THE MODAL NODES

LUKE SKYWALKER'S BELT POUCH

Luke Skywalker

A YOUNG FARMBOY living on the remote desert planet Tatooine, Luke Skywalker yearns to escape the dull routine of his daily chores on his uncle's moisture farm. Luke dreams of becoming a space pilot, but is torn between his desire to enroll in the Academy and his loyalty to his uncle and aunt, who need him on the farm. When Luke discovers a cryptic secret message hidden in one of his new droids, he sets out on a quest and is catapulted into a world of adventure which will at last fulfill his true destiny.

LUKE AND BIGGS DARKLIGHTER

Luke's home is mostly underground, to escape the heat of Tatooine's twin suns. Tunnels connect the main courtyard to the hangar well and the covered garage.

Garage roof

Entrance dome

Salt flats

Courtyard

Cistern cap

Moisture vaporator extracts water vapor from air

Fusion generator supply tanks

Tosche power station in the small town of Anchorhead offers a place for Luke to escape the farm and spend time with his friends— talking, playing electronically-assisted pool, or tinkering with his landspeeder or skyhopper.

Luke first encounters part of the hidden truth about his father when Ben Kenobi gives him his father's Jedi lightsaber. In Luke's hands it flares to life again for the first time in many years.

Droid caller

Tool pouch

Utility belt

Tatooine farm tunic

Light pants

Sandproof leg bindings

Blade stabilizing ring

Blade length adjust

Quick recharge plug

Anakin Skywalker's lightsaber

Activation matrix

AUNT BERU LARS

UNCLE OWEN LARS

Lightsaber

A gift from another era, Luke's lightsaber is the legacy of his father Anakin, a former Jedi Knight of the Old Republic and a warrior who fought in the Clone Wars. A symbol of Luke's destiny, the lightsaber is unlike any other weapon. Luke has a natural ability with the saber and begins to learn rapidly from his mentor Ben Kenobi.

Pitting from desert sand and gravel

Air circulation grille over cooling intakes and exhaust

Grip soles

Power cell

Handgrip

DATA FILE

> Luke's best friend was Biggs Darklighter, who left Tatooine to enlist in the Academy. Biggs graduated with a commission on the freighter *Rand Ecliptic*. Luke is reunited with Biggs on the flight deck of the Rebel base at Yavin 4, where he learns that Biggs has become a Rebel pilot. The friends fly and fight together in the critical attack on the Death Star.

> Sandstorms scour the surface of Tatooine for days at a time, but farm work on the vaporators still has to be done. Luke wears a desert poncho and goggles for protection on windy days.

Model includes decor and enhanced components Luke hopes to get when he can afford them

Emblem Luke would like to add

Pneumatic projectile gun for blasting womp rats

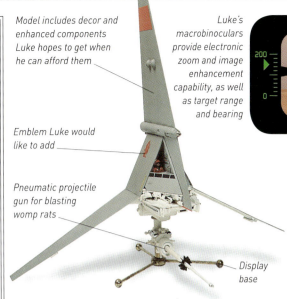

Display base

Luke owns a suborbital T-16 skyhopper (his own model of it is shown above), which he races through the narrow ravines of Beggar's Canyon with his friends, blasting womp rat dens in sheltered hollows. Having narrowly made it through both Diablo Cut and the Stone Needle, Luke has proven himself an excellent pilot. He cannot search for R2-D2 in the skyhopper because his uncle has grounded him for reckless flying.

Luke's macrobinoculars provide electronic zoom and image enhancement capability, as well as target range and bearing

While working on a vaporator, Luke uses his macrobinoculars to observe a space battle between two ships far overhead.

The kitchen of the Lars home is typical of moisture farms, with many moisture-saving devices. The kitchen passage leads up to the dining room, which opens onto the main courtyard.

Luke's Landspeeder

Luke's X-34 landspeeder hovers above the ground, suspended by low-power repulsorlifts which keep the craft floating even when parked. Three turbines boost the repulsor drive effect and jet the speeder across the wide open spaces of the desert. The windshield can be closed to a sealed bubble, but Luke hasn't been able to fix the back half, so he keeps the cockpit open.

LANDSPEEDER SCANNER

R2-D2 appears on the landspeeder scanner

Repulsor drive generators

LANDSPEEDER—SIDE AND REAR

Crash damage

Velocity sensor

Hood panel

Power boost circuits

Duraplex windshield

Steering wheel

Cockpit

Cushioned seats

Storage well

Thrust turbine vent

Turbine mount

Turbine jet exhaust

Repulsor field generator housing

Repulsor vents

Primary repulsor exhaust

Steering turbine engine with cowling removed

Princess Leia Organa

STRONG-WILLED and a woman of action, Princess Leia Organa of Alderaan uses her position in the Galactic Senate as a cover for diplomatic aid to the Rebel Alliance. Able to travel throughout the galaxy on her consular ship *Tantive IV*, Leia brings aid to beleaguered planets and secretly makes connections for the Rebellion. A beautiful and pensive young woman, she understands only too well her crucial position at a fateful time for the galaxy, and she hides her personal feelings behind stern discipline and dedication to her cause. As the adoptive daughter of Viceroy Bail Organa, Leia was trained for her royal position by the finest minds on Alderaan. The Princess was highly educated in martial and political arts in a lifelong preparation for her role.

Stolen Imperial blaster

Symbolic belt worn by Alderaan royalty

Traditional gown of the Alderaan royal family

Travel boots

Twin turbolasers

Primary sensor array

Escape pods

Command bridge

Tantive IV

Serving Leia as it did her father, the *Tantive IV* is a Corellian Corvette, a common ship design seen throughout the galaxy. Blending in anonymously amongst galactic space traffic, so many Corvettes have been converted for smuggling or covert uses that they are often called "Blockade Runners."

While on a secret mission to summon the aid of the Jedi Knight Obi-Wan Kenobi, Leia is trapped on board her diplomatic starship. Knowing she will be captured, she nonetheless fights to the end, and does what she can to ensure that her message will reach Obi-Wan, via R2-D2, even if she herself cannot.

A princess alone within the soulless metal depths of the Death Star, Leia was incarcerated by Darth Vader after her capture. She held firm against every torture.

Princess Leia's influence, royal connections, and diplomatic abilities obtained much of the vital communication and scanning equipment in the Rebel command center on the Fourth Moon of Yavin.

On-duty braids

Rank insignia

Heated vest

White insulated jumpsuit

Boot bindings

Military snow boots

Within the frozen command center of Echo Base, Leia watches the scanners intently for any sign of Imperial detection. Her concerns are always with her people.

Although her background has given her little training in mechanical hardware work, Princess Leia does her best to help with repairs when the *Falcon* is in trouble.

Amidst the fabulous beauty of Cloud City, Leia has only a brief time to share with the *Falcon's* flashy rogue captain before they are all ensnared in Darth Vader's trap.

When Echo Base is discovered and invaded by Imperial forces, Leia inspires the Rebel pilots, staying at her command post and directing the evacuation even when the base begins to collapse around her.

Ice Princess

Trading her ceremonial gown for an insulated jumpsuit, Leia still wears symbolic white as the princess of a lost planet in the corridors of Hoth's Echo Base. As the Alliance faces new challenges, she remains a key command figure, directing deployments and determining key strategic moves, with General Rieekan and other Alliance leaders.

Jabba's Slave

Braving the dangers of Jabba's palace in her quest to rescue Han Solo, Leia knew she could face torture or death if captured. Though she did not anticipate the grueling experience of serving as Jabba's slave girl, she endures her captivity with fierce spirit and keeps ready to turn on Jabba when the time is right.

Slave girl harness

Lashaa silk

Jerba leather boots

Where dozens of professional assassins had failed, Leia succeeds in putting an end to the contemptible crime lord Jabba the Hutt.

Rank insignia

Trusty light target pistol

Rebel Leader

Exposed as a Rebel, Princess Leia's career as a recognized diplomat is over, but she contributes more than ever to the strength of the Alliance. No longer content to be just a great symbol, a leader, and a negotiator, Leia also returns to action in the field, proving that she is still one of the best shots in the Alliance.

DATA FILE

❯ Princess Leia is the youngest person ever to hold a seat in the Galactic Senate. Intelligent and a strong leader, Leia is used to taking charge and making things happen.

❯ Trained in military discipline, techniques, and strategy, Leia is an excellent tactician and an expert shot with a blaster. She virtually never misses.

❯ As princess of Alderaan, Leia is a noble leader of her people; as a senator she represents her entire home planet in the Galactic Senate, stirring much sympathy for the Rebellion. Within the Rebel Alliance the princess is a beloved leader and symbol of hope.

Forest Diplomat

Leia's good spirit and natural gift for diplomacy help her to win the confidence of the Ewoks she meets on Endor. By swapping her combat uniform (right) for clothes they make for her, she helps to win humble allies that will topple the Empire.

Han Solo

MERCENARY PIRATE, smuggler captain, and cocksure braggart, the overly confident Han Solo is a rugged individual of the Galactic Rim. From impoverished beginnings, Solo worked up through petty thievery to gain a commission in the Academy, from which he was later expelled. A Corellian pilot of the finest caliber nonetheless, Solo gained control of his destiny when he won his ship, the *Millennium Falcon*, in the best game of sabacc he ever played. His reputation as a gunfighter matches his renown as captain of the *Falcon*. Reckless and foolhardy, he is also courageous and daring, a match for any adventure.

Customized blaster pistol

Corellian spacer black vest and light shirt

Faced at gunpoint by one of Jabba's minions in the Mos Eisley Cantina, Han Solo keeps his cool and slowly draws his blaster under the table. The regulars could have warned Greedo that Han was the wrong man to threaten. Only one of them would walk away from the table.

Scope

Scope settings and adjustment

Flash suppressor

Enhanced blast delivery circuits

Cooling unit

Final stage collimator

Power pack

Power pack release lever

Trigger

Low-power pulse warning

Power pack

Quick-draw holster

HAN SOLO'S DL-44 PISTOL

Droid caller

Blaster power cell

Captain's pants

Corellian blood stripe

Captain Solo's loyal friend and first mate is the imposing Wookiee Chewbacca. Each has risked his life for the other in many tight situations. Between Han's fast draw and Chewbacca's violent strength, the two are not to be trifled with.

Holster thigh grip

One of Han's regular employers has been the crime lord Jabba the Hutt. When Han had to jettison a cargo to avoid arrest, he incurred Jabba's wrath and was unable to pay him back. This has led to Jabba posting a deadly bounty on Han's head that will haunt him until he resolves the situation.

DATA FILE

› As a child Solo was raised by space gypsies, never knowing who his real parents were. He learned tricks and self-reliance from his adoptive community.

› Solo's last-minute rescue of Luke Skywalker saved the Rebel Alliance and won him one of the highest medals of honor, along with Chewbacca and Luke Skywalker.

Action boots

FALCON QUAD-LASER SCOPE

Upper quad-
laser cannon

Main sensor
rectenna

Starboard
docking ring

Cockpit

Hyperspace
integrator

With the *Falcon* on the run and in need of repairs, Han Solo lands at Bespin to meet the ship's previous owner Lando Calrissian, not knowing for certain how Lando will react.

Han in Carbonite

Trapped in a plot by Darth Vader to ensnare his friend Luke Skywalker, Han Solo is taken to the industrial bowels of Cloud City and flash-frozen in carbonite to test the process meant to immobilize Luke. Carbon-freezing is a way of bonding condensed Tibanna gas for transport, but can be used to keep life forms in suspended animation when the painful process of freezing does not kill them.

Millennium Falcon

This battered and aging YT-1300 light freighter has had a long history in the hands of several captains. Han's extensive modifications to the ship have made it one of the fastest vessels in hyperspace. Even at sublight speeds its velocity and maneuverability are extraordinary for a ship of its class. The *Falcon* sports Imperial military-grade armor, quad-laser cannons, a top-of-the-line sensor rectenna, and many other illegal and customized hot-rod components. The ship serves them as a unique home and powerful workhorse.

Han proves to Leia that there is more to being a scoundrel than having a checkered past. A princess and a guy like him?

Carbonite
frame

Life
system
monitor

Flash-blasted
carbonite
matrix

Carbonite
flux monitor

Han had heard spacers' tales about the legendary titan space slug, but he scoffed at them as nothing more than ghost stories. His narrow escape from the belly of a live space slug restores his distrust in anything being really safe.

Solo, Rebel Leader

After the victory at Yavin, Han eventually accepts a commission as captain in the Rebel Alliance. At frozen Echo Base on Hoth, he volunteers for difficult perimeter patrol duty even though he does not like tauntauns or the cold. Han is a natural leader and serves as an inspiration to many of the troopers around him.

Heavy weather parka

Gas ratio
monitor

Carbonite
integrity
monitor

REBEL SENSOR
PACK

Extensible
antenna

Stentronic
wave monitor

Power
indicator

Range cycle
computer

Power
cells

Stolen Imperial
electrobinoculars

HOTH EQUIPMENT
With their patrol craft paralyzed by the icy cold, the Rebels must survey the snow plains of Hoth with hand-carried gear. Han Solo is an expert at keeping a low profile and seeing others before they see him, and has helped design the Echo Base perimeter survey plan.

Chewbacca
WOOKIEE CO-PILOT

A MIGHTY WOOKIEE from the planet Kashyyyk, Chewbacca was rescued from slavery by Han Solo. Teaming with him to repay the traditional Wookiee life debt, Chewbacca later "adopted" the wayward Corellian and became his best friend. The great Wookiee now uses his mechanical abilities to keep Solo's heavily modified spaceship flying, and serves as both a fiercely loyal co-pilot and a trusty fellow adventurer. Chewie enjoys a good fight and likes the action that Solo gets them into, but sometimes acts as his partner's conscience.

Han Solo and Chewbacca make a dauntless pair of spacers, following adventure where it leads them. The two fight well together, knowing each other's strengths and relying on each other's abilities. Han's ego may get them into trouble or Chewie's temper may start fights, but the two of them together know when to blast 'em and when to run.

Although the *Millennium Falcon* cockpit is small for his great frame, Chewbacca is at ease with the myriad controls and co-pilots the ship with confidence. Deferring to Han's outstanding marksmanship, Chewie usually flies the ship while Han mans a gun turret during pursuit space combat.

Padding

Ammo case lid

Quarrel

Insulated lining

Six-shell ammo case

Detonator pin

Energy shell flare material

Shell casing

Accelerator lock surface

QUARREL

BOWCASTER AMMUNITION
The traditional Wookiee bowcaster uses a magnetic accelerator to fire explosive quarrels, which are enveloped in a penetrating energy shell as they are fired. The bowcaster has a range of 50 meters and requires immense strength to cock.

Blue eyes

Sensitive nose

Bandolier

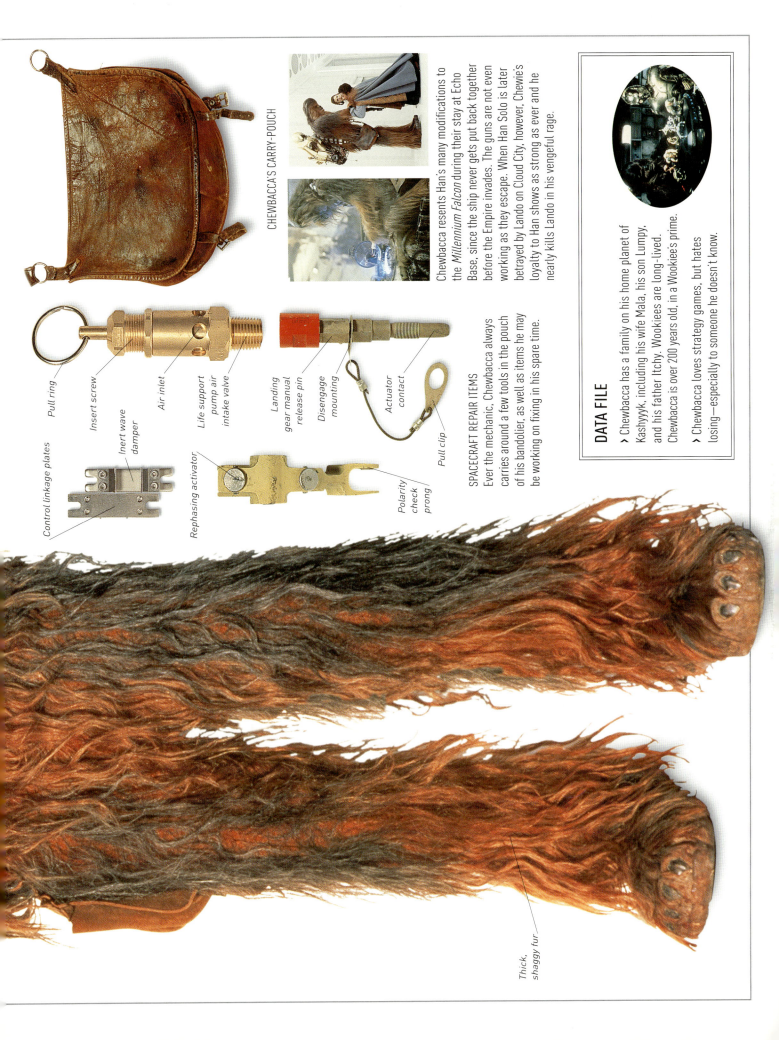

CHEWBACCA'S CARRY-POUCH

Chewbacca resents Han's many modifications to the *Millennium Falcon* during their stay at Echo Base, since the ship never gets put back together before the Empire invades. The guns are not even working as they escape. When Han Solo is later betrayed by Lando on Cloud City, however, Chewie's loyalty to Han shows as strong as ever and he nearly kills Lando in his vengeful rage.

Pull ring

Insert screw

Inert wave damper

Air inlet

Life support pump air intake valve

Landing gear manual release pin

Disengage mounting

Actuator contact

Control linkage plates

Rephasing activator

Pull clip

Polarity check prong

SPACECRAFT REPAIR ITEMS
Ever the mechanic, Chewbacca always carries around a few tools in the pouch of his bandolier, as well as items he may be working on fixing in his spare time.

DATA FILE

> Chewbacca has a family on his home planet of Kashyyyk, including his wife Mala, his son Lumpy, and his father Itchy. Wookiees are long-lived. Chewbacca is over 200 years old, in a Wookiee's prime.

> Chewbacca loves strategy games, but hates losing—especially to someone he doesn't know.

Thick, shaggy fur

C-3PO
PROTOCOL DROID

IN A GALAXY filled with countless cultures and languages, protocol droids assist their masters in matters of etiquette, custom, and translation, assuring that intercultural relations proceed peacefully. C-3PO is fluent in over six million forms of communication and has a strongly programmed desire to see things run smoothly, but neither of these traits prepared him for the turbulent events he would face. Transported into a world of adventure, this pragmatic character is often overwhelmed by the extraordinary action around him, but he faithfully serves his masters.

Keeping an eye out for trouble: 3PO never seems to get through his adventures completely intact. Fortunately, his sturdy components are easily repaired and reassembled.

Infra-red

Neon

Human

MYRIAD VISUAL SYSTEM - MK. 2

Photoreceptors

Photoreceptor brace

Vocabulator

Language memory discs

TRANLANG III COMMUNICATION MODULE (ENLARGED)

Audio sensor

Olfactory sensor

Microwave emitter/sensor

Logic function computer

Memory shielding rings

Audio output modifier

Energy transducer

Speech generator

Self-sealing internal system linkages

Movement motivator

Attachment clamps

LOCOMOTORY SYSTEMS CONTROL INTERFACE (ENLARGED)

Restraining bolt mount

Wrist linkage

Multi-system connection wires

Primary power coupler outlet

Power buscable C

Pelvic servo motor

Wave harmonizer

Primary power coupler

Intermotor actuating coupler

Powerbus linkage cables

Retainer connector

RECHARGE COUPLING SYSTEM

TERTIARY LIMB MOTOR

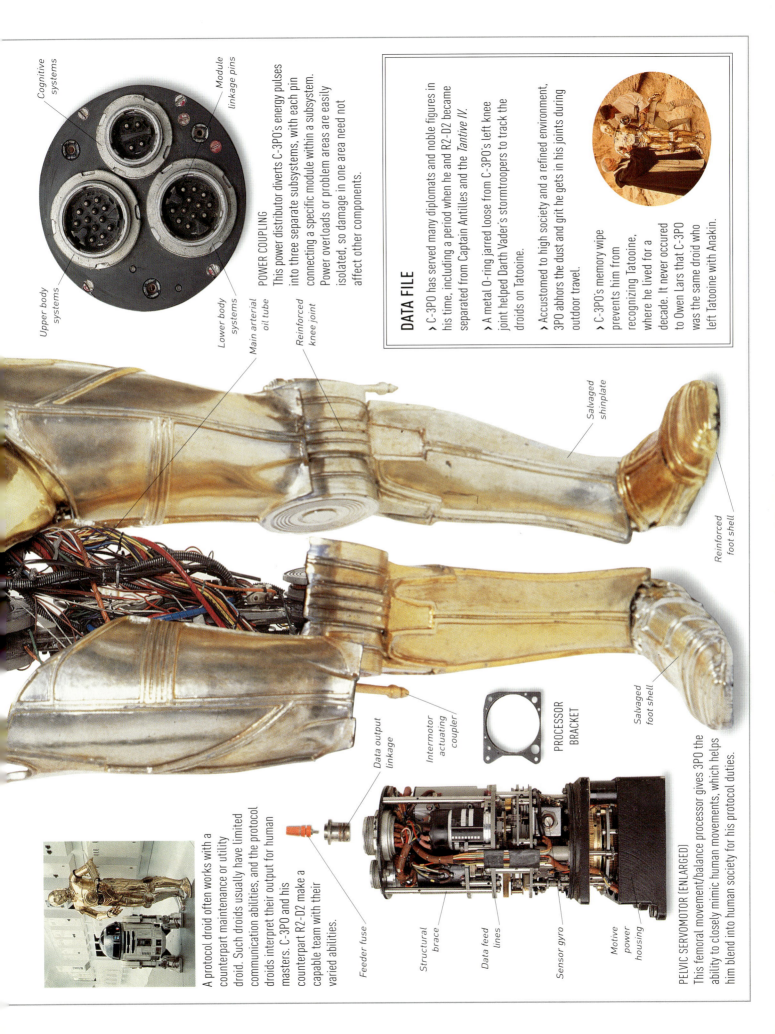

Cognitive systems

Module linkage pins

Upper body systems

Lower body systems

Main arterial oil tube

Reinforced knee joint

POWER COUPLING
This power distributor diverts C-3PO's energy pulses into three separate subsystems, with each pin connecting a specific module within a subsystem. Power overloads or problem areas are easily isolated, so damage in one area need not affect other components.

DATA FILE

➤ C-3PO has served many diplomats and noble figures in his time, including a period when he and R2-D2 became separated from Captain Antilles and the *Tantive IV*.

➤ A metal 0-ring jarred loose from C-3PO's left knee joint helped Darth Vader's stormtroopers to track the droids on Tatooine.

➤ Accustomed to high society and a refined environment, 3PO abhors the dust and grit he gets in his joints during outdoor travel.

➤ C-3PO's memory wipe prevents him from recognizing Tatooine, where he lived for a decade. It never occured to Owen Lars that C-3PO was the same droid who left Tatooine with Anakin.

Salvaged shinplate

Reinforced foot shell

Data output linkage

Intermotor actuating coupler

PROCESSOR BRACKET

Salvaged foot shell

A protocol droid often works with a counterpart maintenance or utility droid. Such droids usually have limited communication abilities, and the protocol droids interpret their output for human masters. C-3PO and his counterpart R2-D2 make a capable team with their varied abilities.

Feeder fuse

PELVIC SERVOMOTOR (ENLARGED)
This femoral movement/balance processor gives 3PO the ability to closely mimic human movements, which helps him blend into human society for his protocol duties.

Structural brace

Data feed lines

Sensor gyro

Motive power housing

R2-D2

ASTROMECH DROID

DESIGNED AS a sophisticated computer repair and information retrieval droid, R2-D2 is a highly useful astromech unit filled with apparatus of all sorts. His long history of adventures has given him distinct personality and quirkiness. R2 exhibits a strong motivation to succeed in his assigned tasks, displaying stubborn determination and inventiveness that are extraordinary for a utility droid. A protocol droid like C-3PO must translate his electronic beeps and whistles for human masters, but that doesn't stop R2 from trying to communicate anyway, and he usually manages to get his points across, even without an interpreter. Highly loyal, R2 is never reluctant to risk damage or destruction to help his masters and accomplish missions.

When R2-D2 disappears into a swamp on Dagobah, Luke thinks he may have lost his companion for good until R2's periscope pops out of the murky water.

Princess Leia entrusted R2-D2 with the stolen Death Star plans and her urgent message to Obi-Wan Kenobi, which R2 faithfully found a way to deliver. Hologram recording and projection is one of R2-D2's standard capabilities.

An on-board R2 unit is a vital component of the Incom T-65 X-wing. The droid's in-flight adjustments allow for optimum performance. Most pilots would want to use the available droid in the best condition, but Luke Skywalker grows attached to R2-D2 and chooses the droid to accompany him in the attack on the Death Star.

Mounting bracket

Extensible rod

Information buffer

Magnetic lock

COMPUTER INTERFACE ARM
One of several kinds of interface arms, this unit allows R2 to communicate with computer systems for information exchange and command implementation.

Hydraulic casing

Gripping servomotor

Pincer claw

Grasping sensor

GRASPING ARM
This gripper arm enables R2-D2 to manipulate objects and to adjust power routings on board Luke's X-wing.

Insulated casing

Overload breaker

Contact prongs

Power regulator

Charge capacitator

POWER CHARGE ARM
A power output arm allows R2-D2 to recharge dead machinery or pulse electricity through damaged circuits for diagnostic tests.

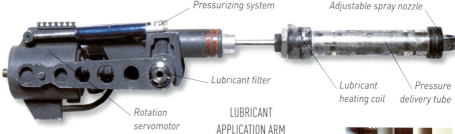

Pressurizing system

Adjustable spray nozzle

Lubricant filter

Lubricant heating coil

Pressure delivery tube

Rotation servomotor

LUBRICANT APPLICATION ARM

Arm Extensions

R2-D2's extension arms include everything from welding tips to cutter devices, clamps, and magnetic depolarizing leads. Many such devices are built into his various compartments, and an interchangeable component design allows him to be equipped with still others for special tasks.

DATA FILE

❯ Durable and strongly built, R2-D2 has been around even longer than his counterpart C-3PO.

❯ R2-D2 resorts to innovative deceit when necessary, which makes 3PO throw up his hands in dismay. One of R2's deceptions began all of Luke's adventures.

R2-D2 uses his fire extinguisher inventively to conceal his friends from attacking stormtroopers.

Life-scan mesh

Primary photo receptor and radar eye

Data card input

Inert alloy plate

Processor state indicator

Logic function display

Holographic projector

Overload heat vent

Signal amplifier

Sensory input head

MOTIVATOR HOUSING AND VENT

HOLOGRAM PROJECTOR BULB

Head rotation ring

Computer interface and lubricant application arms compartment

Spacecraft linkage data slot

Spacecraft linkage and control arms

Reinforced rod

Actuating coupler

Acoustic signaler

Hydraulic extension

System ventilation

Stored experiences

Main logic processor connection

MEMORY CHIP

SCANNER ANTENNA

Charge arm compartment

MAIN POWER COUPLING

Systems diagnostic input receptors

Interference pulse stabilizers

Grasping arm compartment

Polarity sink

Heat exhaust

Recharge power coupling

Durasteel shell

Astromech units are standard droid types, and Jabba's personnel found a fitting that would allow R2-D2 to serve drinks on board Jabba's sail barge.

Locomotion power cells

Powerbus cables

Third tread (retractable)

Motorized all-terrain treads

Lando Calrissian

THE DASHING Baron Administrator of Cloud City has a past that few on Bespin would suspect. As a rogue and con artist, Lando built his early fortunes from modest beginnings, becoming a daring smuggler captain with a good head for business and a bad habit of gambling. He flew the *Millennium Falcon* for years before losing the ship to Han Solo in a sabacc match. The same game later won Lando control of the fabulous gas mining colony on Bespin. As the flamboyant leader of Cloud City, Lando combines his sense of style with a new-found sense of responsibility and has come to enjoy his role as Baron Administrator.

Winning smile

Borrowed Rebel blaster

Tarelle sel-weave shirt

Baron Administrator state belt

Aeien silk lining

Royal emblems

Baron's cape

Handmade Liwari shoes

Cloud City

Suspended high above the core of the gas giant Bespin, Cloud City was once the headquarters of great royal leaders. The city's glorious past has filled the skyline with monumental majesty and ethereal beauty. The city is supported on a single giant column which stems from a processing reactor at its base. In the city's hollow air shaft core are gigantic directional vanes that control the facility's location in space.

Cloud City is home to industrious citizens and advanced technology. Facilities throughout the city process for export the rare anti-gravitational tibanna gas from the exotic atmosphere of Bespin.

Calrissian is forced to betray Han Solo and his friends to Darth Vader in order to preserve Cloud City's freedom. When Lando learns that Vader has no intention of keeping the bargain, he plots a rescue and escape with his aide Lobot.

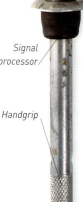

Broadcast antenna

Microphone

Signal processor

Handgrip

COMLINK

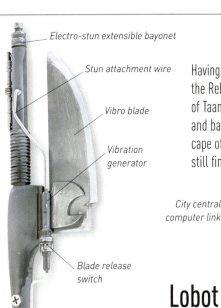

Electro-stun extensible bayonet

Stun attachment wire

Vibro blade

Vibration generator

Blade release switch

Grip

Blade/electro-stun power unit

Reinforced lance pole

VIBRO-AXE POLEARM

General Lando

Having become a renegade on the run from the Empire, Lando fell in with the Rebels after leaving Cloud City. His penetrating judgment at the Battle of Taanab won Lando promotion within the ranks, and the former con artist and baron became a general within the Alliance. He once more wears a cape of honor and authority. Grown beyond his self-centered past, Lando still finds adventure but now contributes his abilities to a greater cause.

Rank insignia

Dress cape

Rank plaque

Alliance general's uniform

Sidearm blaster

Wrist comlink

City central computer link

Lobot

Equipped with cybernetic implants, the Chief Administrative Aide of Cloud City keeps in direct contact with the city's central computer. Able to monitor a vast array of details at once, Lobot is an ideal assistant to Lando Calrissian. Lobot takes great satisfaction in making Cloud City a well-run success.

Cyborg unit

By turning against the Imperial forces of Darth Vader, Lando loses everything he has built as Baron Administrator of Cloud City. Racing through the corridors of the city with Leia and Chewbacca, Lando witnesses Boba Fett lift off with Han Solo, and barely escapes with his life from the city he once ruled.

Disguised as a lowly skiff guard at Jabba's palace, Lando braves the very heart of danger to rescue Han Solo. His old con man skills are put to good use, and no one at the palace ever suspects him until it is too late.

DATA FILE

> Using a comlink and his security code, Lando can address all parts of Cloud City from any central computer terminal.

> Lando uses an old underworld contact on Tatooine to secure a guard job at Jabba's palace.

Obi-Wan Kenobi

JEDI IN EXILE

FAR OUT in the remote Jundland wastes lives the hermit Ben Kenobi. Ben is a figure of mystery to the Tatooine settlers, dismissed by many as a crazy wizard. In truth Kenobi is a Jedi Knight, a great warrior of the Old Republic who fought in the Clone Wars. One of Kenobi's students turned to the dark side of the Force, betraying the Jedi and assisting the rise of the Emperor. Crushed by his failure with the man who became Darth Vader, Kenobi retreated to Tatooine, watching over the young Luke Skywalker and waiting for the time to reveal Luke's birthright as the son of a Jedi. Kenobi's powers make him a threat to the Empire even in his elder years.

Hooded cloak

Jedi robes

In accordance with Jedi philosophy, Kenobi lives simply. In his hut are only a few scant reminders of his former life and great exploits. It is here that Kenobi gives Luke his father's lightsaber.

Hovering training remotes are used by Jedi and also by gunfighters to sharpen reflexes and develop coordination. They can be set to varying degrees of aggressiveness and their shock rays adjusted from harmless to painful.

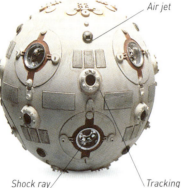

Air jet

Shock ray emitter

TRAINING REMOTE

Tracking sensor

On board the Death Star, Kenobi uses his technical knowledge and Jedi mind powers to disable a crucial tractor beam without being noticed. This is his first return to such heroic action in many years.

Even after he is struck down by Vader, Kenobi returns in spirit to guide Luke on his path to becoming a Jedi. On Hoth and near death, Luke sees Kenobi just before being rescued by Han Solo.

It is Kenobi who first awakens Jedi abilities in Luke and begins to train him, but Luke can learn from him only briefly before Kenobi faces his final lightsaber duel. Afterward, as Luke learns the ways of the Force, he is able to meet Ben again in spirit.

DATA FILE

> Ben Kenobi once rescued Luke when the boy had become lost in the Tatooine wilderness with his friend Windy. In spite of this, Owen Lars forbade Kenobi from ever coming near their farm again.

> Luke Skywalker returns to the home of Ben Kenobi to build his own lightsaber after losing his father's in the battle on Cloud City.

Yoda

SKYWALKER'S TEACHER

NOT TO BE JUDGED by his small size, the wise Jedi Master Yoda is very powerful with the Force. At almost 900, his years of contemplation and training have given him deep insight and profound abilities. One of his greatest challenges is the training of Luke Skywalker, who arrives on Dagobah an impatient would-be Jedi. In the short time he has with Luke, Yoda must instill in him the faith, peace, and harmony with the Force that will fulfill Luke's potential and guard him from the dark path of temptation, anger, and evil. To his final student, Yoda imparts the heart of the ancient Jedi traditions that are the galaxy's last hope.

Jedi robes

Through the Force, Luke Skywalker is able to see his mentors Yoda and Obi-Wan, as well as a youthful apparition of his father Anakin, all finally at peace due to Luke's heroic efforts. United in the Force, their Jedi spirits are restored and complete.

On Dagobah, Yoda uses his attunement with the natural world to live peacefully on the resources around him. His gimer stick, for example, serves as a walking staff as well as a source of pleasant gimer juice, which can be chewed out of the bark.

HEALING MOTHER-ROCK

Dagobah

A remote planet of swamps and mists, inhospitable Dagobah hides a tremendous variety of life forms, including gnarl trees, butcherbugs, and swamp slugs. This inhospitable setting provides a good hiding place in the dark days of the Empire.

YARUM SEED
tea-making variety

MUSHROOM SPORES

GALLA SEEDS

SOHLI BARK

Sensitive ears

Green skin

Gimer stick

Tridactyl feet

Yoda spends his days in meditation, seeing ever deeper into the infinite tapestry that is the living vitality of the Force. Like Obi-Wan, he hides behind an assumed identity of harmless craziness. Yoda uses this persona to test Luke upon his arrival on Dagobah. As Obi-Wan once told Luke, "Your eyes can deceive you. Don't trust them."

DATA FILE

> Yoda's house expresses his oneness with nature, using no technological appliances or fittings. All the furnishings in the house of clay, sticks, and stones were handcrafted by Yoda himself.

> In the days before the sinister Empire, Yoda held a seat within the Jedi high council on the Republic's capital world of Coruscant.

Darth Vader

A GRIM, FORBIDDING FIGURE, Darth Vader stalks the corridors of the Imperial Navy. Once regarded as mad human wreckage, with the increasing favor of the Emperor, Vader has risen in power and influence to become a much-feared military commander. Grand Moff Tarkin was one of the few who recognized Vader's capabilities in spite of his bizarre appearance and eccentric conduct, and as Tarkin's right-hand man, Vader attained a new level of respect amongst the upper echelons of the Imperial military. Unable to survive without the constant life support provided by his suit, Vader is nonetheless a powerful figure whose knowledge of the dark side of the Force makes him unnerving and dangerous.

Magnetic
sensor pits

Speech projector
and respiratory
intake

Respiratory vent

Neck vertebra
replaced
with metal

Outer
cloak

Vision enhancement
receptors

Armored breast plate to
shield badly injured chest

Cybernetic replacement
internal organs

Control chestplate

Control function
connectors

Vader is hardly pleased when his pursuit of Princess Leia's starship delivers him to the orbit of Tatooine, his despised homeworld, where he last saw his mother. As Leia is entirely unaware of her true heritage, Vader fails to realize he has captured his own daughter.

Vader allows no one to assist him with his accoutrements. In a special isolation chamber, mechanical arms assist in the removal and replacement of certain suit components.

Artificial
cyborg
lower arm

CHESTPLATE
Vader's life support systems are monitored and controlled through this central panel of chestplate controls on his suit. Slots allow the insertion of diagnostic cards for periodic system checkouts, while switch panels allow function modification.

System function
indicator

Secondary system
function box

Control activator; only when this is pushed
will Vader's chestplate controls work

Electromagnetic
clasp

DARTH VADER'S BELT

Synthetic belt
strap

Primary system
function box

Armored boots binding cyborg elements to flesh

DATA FILE

> Over time, Vader has advanced in his ability to manipulate the dark side of the Force, and has used it to sustain his own damaged body as well as to persuade opponents of his will. Under the Emperor's tutelage, Vader learns to kill with mere suggestion.

> Despite the fact that much of his body was replaced by machine components after his battle against Obi-Wan Kenobi on Mustafar, Darth Vader retains an incredibly high count of midi-chlorians.

> Vader incurs the wrath of high officers by piloting his own fighter into combat.

Vader plotted with the Emperor to sway Luke to the dark side. In an intense lightsaber battle, Vader tempted Luke with the proposal that the two of them join to overthrow the Emperor. Where Vader's loyalties really stood at this time is lost in the darkness filling his soul.

Body heat regulators

Outer helmet locking surface

Multiple power cells

Hermetic seal

Power distributor

Helmet air pump

Electrical system radiators

Neck support

Hermetic seal

Voice processor

Nutrient feed tube

Air processing filter

Primary environmental sensor

INTERIOR OF VADER'S HELMET

Vader's helmet is the most important part of his life support suit, connecting with a flat backpack to cycle air in and out of Vader's broken lungs and keeping his hideously damaged skull in shape.

Anakin Skywalker

The horror and tragedy of Darth Vader are revealed when he tells Luke Skywalker "I am your father." Vader hopes to bring Luke down the same dark path of hate and anger that destroyed Anakin Skywalker. Instead he finds that Luke is committed to finding redemption for his father in spite of all that Vader has become.

Imperial Leaders

THE EMPEROR'S WILL is enforced by the might of the Imperial Space Navy and its assault forces. Imperial military commanders carry out the orders of the Emperor and hold the true positions of power in the New Order. The price for failure can be death, but ambition for the highest posts keeps competition fierce amongst officers. While bureaucracy and political whims can place incapable men in high posts, many of the Empire's commanders are formidable military talents in a system that values ruthless efficiency.

TRACKING MONITOR
This Death Star tracking monitor shows the Fourth Moon of Yavin emerging from behind the planet itself into firing range.

Superlaser

Exhaust port

THE FIRST DEATH STAR
The Death Star contains a hypermatter reactor that can generate enough power to destroy an entire planet. Invulnerable to large-scale assault, the space station has a fatal weakness in a small thermal exhaust port (connecting directly to the main reactor) which can be bombed by a small fighter craft.

Docking bays

SUPERLASER TARGETING DISPLAY

DEATH STAR GUNNERS
Obeying the orders of their superiors, gunnery crew leaders ensure that the titanic energies of the Death Star laser systems do not overload or hit phase imbalances that would cause huge internal explosions.

DEATH STAR GUNNER'S HELMET

Aboard the original Death Star, this conference room can project holographic tactical readouts for evaluation by Tarkin and his Imperial strategists.

Grand Moff Tarkin

Governor of the Imperial Outland Regions, Grand Moff Wilhuff Tarkin conceives the horrific Death Star superweapon as part of his doctrine of Rule by Fear. The Imperial Outlands contain systems too scattered to police effectively, but the fear of the Death Star will subjugate systems across the galaxy.

Antenna

Transceiver

Shielded lens

Imperial Navy emblem

Neutral-alloy helmet

Officer tunic

Imperial officer's disc

Rank insignia plaque

Imperial code cylinder

ADMIRAL PIETT

Officer's disc

ADMIRAL OZZEL

General Veers

General Maximillian Veers masterminds the devastating Imperial assault on Echo Base, commanding the action in person within the lead walker cockpit. A cunning and capable individual, Veers is a model Imperial officer.

Tunic

CAPTAIN NEEDA

MOFF JERJERROD

Emperor Palpatine

IN THE LAST DAYS of the Republic, Senator Palpatine used deception to become elected Supreme Chancellor of the Galactic Senate. Once in office he appointed himself Emperor. He declared martial law throughout the galaxy and began to rule through the military forces of the newly-created Imperial Navy. Palpatine affected the simple clothing of a simple man, but drew his powers of persuasion and control from the blackest depths of the dark side of the Force. While the Force has twisted his face, it has also sustained him beyond his years, and even in his old age the Emperor remains a figure of terrible power.

Hood to hide face

Simple cloak

The Emperor's ceremonial arrivals are attended by thousands of massed stormtroopers and air parades of fighter wings.

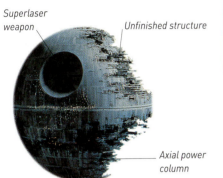

Superlaser weapon

Unfinished structure

Axial power column

THE SECOND DEATH STAR
The Emperor conceived the second Death Star as a colossal trap, which would use a false image of vulnerability to lure the Rebel fleet into fatal combat.

Coruscant headwear

IMPERIAL SHUTTLE

On board the second Death Star, the Emperor's throne room surveys the stars from atop a high isolation tower.

Imperial Dignitaries

The Emperor's favor can elevate individuals to positions of fantastic galactic power. High officials owe their posts to Palpatine's whim, and form a society of twisted sycophants and back-stabbers.

Emperor uses cane because he pretends to be weak, not because he needs it

DATA FILE

› Mysterious and fanatically loyal Imperial Royal Guards protect the Emperor wherever he travels.

› Imperial Royal Guards are so highly trained in deadly arts that their chosen weapon is not a blaster but a vibro-active force pike, which they use with lightning swiftness to inflict very precise and lethal wounds.

Imperial Stormtroopers

MADE UP OF CLONES, as well as human recruits, Imperial Stormtroopers are first-strike units sent into critical combat situations in support of both the Imperial Star Fleet and the Imperial Army. Highly disciplined and completely loyal to the Emperor, stormtroopers carry out their orders without hesitation and without regard to their own lives. These grimly anonymous troopers turn the might of their training and weaponry on any opposition to the Empire with utterly ruthless efficiency. Shielded in white space armor worn over a body glove, stormtroopers are protected from harsh environments, projectile and impact weapons, and glancing blaster bolts. Equipped with the finest and most powerful arms and equipment, they are the most trusted and most effective troops in the Imperial military, and the most deeply feared opponents of the Rebel fighters.

While Imperial Army or Navy forces may be assigned to keep order, stormtroopers are sent in to crush initial resistance and do the toughest fighting. Stormtrooper boarding parties are systematic and professional in taking charge of a captured ship.

Body glove

Plastoid composite armor

Thermal detonator

Utility belt

Energy sinks absorb blast energy

Blaster holster

Suit systems power cells

Short-range combat pistol

Manual suit seal and environmental controls

Blaster power cell container

Reinforced alloy plate ridge

Sniper position knee protector plate

Combat de-ionizer

Positive-grip boots

Cooling fins

Folding three-position stock

Heat vents

UTILITY BELT TOOLS
Standard-issue equipment in the utility belt includes power packs, energy rations, and a compact tool kit. The belt can carry additional gear such as a grappling hook, comlink, macrobinoculars, handcuff binders, or other items such as this combat de-ionizer.

Stormtrooper Blaster

The E-11 BlasTech Standard Imperial Sidearm combines excellent range with lethal firepower in a compact and rugged design. A standard power cell carries enough energy for 100 shots. Replacement cells are carried in a trooper utility belt. Plasma gas cartridges last for over 500 shots and the unit features an advanced cooling system for superior fire-delivery performance. A folding three-position stock converts the weapon to a rifle configuration for sustained long-distance firing.

Often deployed and paraded in overwhelming numbers, the stormtrooper legions are adept at manipulating the psychology of dominance, shielded in the eerie anonymity of their armor.

CODE
TRANSMITTER

STORMTROOPER OFFICER'S CAP

Officer's disc

BELT BUCKLE

OFFICER'S RANK PLAQUES

Series code

Pocket clip

Data interface

CODE CYLINDERS

Reinforced helmet

Broadband communications antenna

Audio pickup

Stormtrooper Officers

In non-combat situations, stormtrooper officers wear distinctive black tunics and caps. Their insignia—officer's discs, rank plaques, and code cylinders—conform to the standards of the Imperial Navy. Code cylinders allow officers access to secure areas and computer systems. All stormtrooper officers are proven soldiers, and in combat they wear body armor like any other trooper. Officers in field units may wear colored shoulder pauldrons as high-visibility rank indicators.

Range-finding sight

Accessory mounting rail

Setting adjust

Gas cartridge cap

Power cell

Energy ration

Blast energy sink

Safety catch

Low-power pulse indicator

Magnatomic adhesion grip

In battle, stormtroopers are disciplined to ignore casualties within their own ranks. Notice is only taken from a tactical standpoint. They are never distracted by emotional responses.

DATA FILE

> A power pack and pressurized gas system in the stormtrooper armor backplate allows a trooper to survive even in the vacuum of space for limited periods. For extended exposure to open space, troopers wear space backpacks with extended life-support capacity.

> Stormtrooper armor is impervious to projectile weapons and blast shrapnel. It may be pierced by a direct blaster bolt, but will deflect glancing bolts and reduce damage from bolts absorbed.

STORMTROOPER ARMOR
Every component of a stormtrooper's armor and equipment is manufactured to the highest standards in the Empire. Their armor lasts indefinitely and may still be found half-buried at decades-old battle sites.

Stormtrooper Equipment

WHILE THE BRUTAL TRAINING and intense conditioning of stormtroopers account for much of their power and effectiveness, Imperial-issue stormtrooper equipment is also vital in making them the galaxy's most dreaded soldiers. Field troops carry gear such as pouches of extra ammunition (power packs and blaster gas cartridges) and comprehensive survival kits. Standard backpack sets can adapt troopers to extreme climates or even the vacuum of space. Component construction allows standard backpack frames to be filled with gear suited to specific missions, which may include micro-vaporator water-gathering canteens, augmented cooling modules, or a wide variety of base camp and field operative equipment.

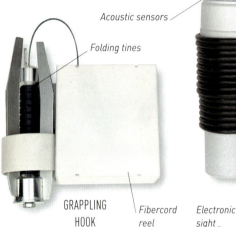

With high-powered backpack communications gear, troopers in Mos Eisley alerted orbiting Star Destroyers to intercept the escaping *Millennium Falcon*.

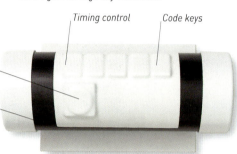

Under able officers like Commander Praji, stormtrooper teams adapt to their environments. The unpredictable sandstorms of Tatooine can immobilize landing craft, but native dewback lizards carry search parties equipped with desert gear through any conditions.

Timing control
Code keys
Detach control
Axidite shell

Comlink

The hand-held comlink supplements a stormtrooper's built-in helmet transmitter/receiver system with improved range and communication security. Comlink sets can be tuned with sophisticated encryption algorithms to work only with each other. Within or near Imperial bases, comlink signals are boosted and relayed automatically for optimal transmission.

Acoustic sensors
Folding tines

GRAPPLING HOOK
Fibercord reel

Thermal Detonator

Stormtroopers are usually issued a thermal detonator, carried at the back of the belt. Controls to set arming, timing, and blast intensity are not labelled so that enemy troops cannot use the powerful explosives if they are captured. While these detonators would not normally be used against intruders on board an Imperial ship or battle station, troopers carry their full set of standard equipment at all times to maintain combat readiness and familiarity with the feel of their gear.

Electronic sight
Rangefinder

BLASTECH DLT-20A LASER RIFLE

Firing capacitor
Cooling vents
Galven circuitry barrel
Power charge system
Magnatomic adhesion grip

Laser Rifle

In field combat situations, the standard Imperial sidearm offers insufficient accuracy at long range. Field troops are issued blaster rifles, which improve the consistency and accuracy of blaster bolt trajectory by incorporating additional collimating rings and longer conduits of galven circuitry. Imperial blaster rifles are extremely rugged weapons, which give Imperial troops a deadly edge in battle. They are much prized on the black market.

DATA FILE

> Stormtrooper backpack gear can include boosted field communication sets, mortar launchers, and equipment for establishing security perimeters.

> Squad leaders, who lead units of seven troopers, wear orange shoulder pauldrons.

Activator

Small power packs plug into standard stormtrooper gear, including standard helmets and back plates as well as communication sets and other field equipment. Complex circuitry extracts the maximum power from the cell.

4 layer construction

Outer plastoid composite armor

Inner insulator

Anti-laser mesh

Magnetic shielding layer

Comtech Series IV speaker uses three-phase sonic filtering for clear sound

Atmospheric cycling unit

Stormtrooper Helmet

There are a number of different models of Imperial stormtrooper standard issue helmets, incorporating various specialized components and changing over time with new developments. In this model, enhanced optical equipment creates holographic images of the surrounding terrain, shielding the eye from excessive brightness and offering vision through many barriers such as smoke, darkness, and fire. Optical equipment in trooper helmets can range from simple eye lenses to these elaborate vision processors. The helmets are cooled and atmosphere-processed to keep the trooper operating at peak efficiency at all times.

Padding

Power cell

Atmosphere intake and processing unit

Used air exhaust

Voice filtering unit

Comlink microphone

Artificial air intake

Mouth plate

Artificial air supply nozzles

123

Specialist Stormtroopers

FOR ANY MILITARY SITUATION there is an appropriate class of Imperial soldier, well-equipped for environments that would challenge the standard stormtrooper. Certain Imperial troopers are selected at an early stage for specialization and conditioned with appropriate knowledge and psychological training. Once specialized, their psychological conditioning to their particular identity is so strong that a trooper almost never wishes to change his division.

Helmet

Polarized snow goggles

Breath warmer cover

Chest plate

Imperial sidearm

Wrist comlink

Heated pants

Insulating belt cape

Legs less heavily armored, for mobility

Rugged ice boots

The E-Web heavy repeating blaster can be broken down into its component parts and carried into difficult snow terrain or through restricted ice passages by a crew of only a few troopers. With weaponry such as this, specialized troopers can destroy any advantage the Rebels hope to gain from unusual terrain.

Adjustable attachment straps

Blast armor

Reinforced blast plate

External temperature monitor

Communication controls

Identity chip

Suit heater controls

Power cell monitor

SNOWTROOPER CHEST PLATE

Communications unit

Heater

Heater liquid pump

Power indicator

Accessory power outlet

Surplus power indicator

Homing beacon

SNOWTROOPER BACKPACK

Heavy-duty power cell

Rations storage compartment

Snowtrooper

Equipped with breath heaters under their face masks, snowtroopers are self-sufficient mobile combat elements. Their backpacks and suit systems keep them warm and exceptionally mobile for environments of ice and snow. They can survive for two weeks in deeply frozen environments on suit battery power alone.

The ground troops of General Veers' Blizzard Force on Hoth find themselves accompanied at the Echo Base invasion by the extraordinary figure of Darth Vader. Vader oversees the occupation of the base with the front line of the assault group.

Terrain sensor

Guidance vanes mounting strut

Forward guidance repulsor field directional vanes

Speeder bike

The light repulsorlift Imperial speeder bike carries one or two riders at high velocities for reconnaissance and anti-personnel missions. An unusual turbine repulsorlift makes the bike stable even in extreme maneuvers. Forward-reaching repulsor fields help thread it through obstacles like trees, but their guidance must be used carefully because they are not strong enough to deflect the bike away from obstacles on their own.

In the dense forests of Endor, biker scouts patrol the perimeters of the Imperial shield generator and its garrison, wary and watchful for troublesome forest creatures or terrorist infiltrators. Working in units of two or four, they coordinate their efforts for superior surveillance coverage.

Electro-magnetic vision enhancement visor

Boosted comlink system for long-range communication

Body glove

Power unit backpack also stores gear

Scout Trooper

Scout troopers are equipped for high maneuverability and long periods without support. Trained to an unusual degree of independence for Imperial personnel, scout troopers are nonetheless conditioned to work with partners wherever possible. Scout troopers are armored only on the head and upper body. They carry food supplies, micro-cords, and other gear that allows them to reach and silently infiltrate almost any objective, far from resupply by Imperial forces.

Survival rations

Survival kit

Acceleration handgrip

Power management setting

Repulsor guide settings

Steering lever

Tracking sensor

Repulsor drive

Braking linkage

Steering sensitivity adjust

Brake pedal

Turbine repulsorlift

Guidance linkage

Phase amplifier

Targeting scope

DATA FILE

> Other specialized Imperial trooper divisions include flying airtroopers, liquid-borne seatroopers, tunneling underminers, and Magma troopers who crush revolts on volcanic mining worlds.

> Scout troopers have motion sensors and enhanced macrobinocular viewplates allowing them to see energy emissions, night vision, and designated target magnification.

Short-range laser emitter

Grip retainer guard

Mini gas cell

SCOUT TROOPER BLASTER

Imperial Pilots

IMPERIAL FIGHTER PILOTS are an elite group within the Imperial naval forces. Only ten percent of those accepted into training graduate with commissions. Through their intense psychological conditioning, pilots are entirely dedicated to target destruction and know that their mission comes above all other concerns, including those of personal survival and aid to threatened wingmen. Each pilot knows he is expendable. TIE pilots are trained to regard the TIE craft as the most expressive instrument of Imperial military will, and they exult in their role, taking pride in their total dependence on higher authority.

Reinforced flight helmet

Ship-linked communi-cations

Gas transfer hose

Life support pack

Vacuum g-suit

Air scrubber

Energy-shielded fabric

Positive gravity pressure boots

TARGETING READOUTS
TIE targeting systems are superior to anything available to Rebel fighters. The advanced readouts of these Seinar systems track targets in high resolution.

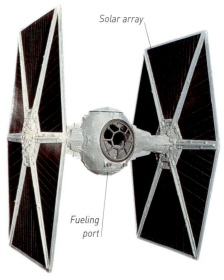

Solar array

Fueling port

TIE Fighter

The standard TIE fighter carries no deflector shield or hyperdrive equipment and employs high-performance ion engines energized by solar array "wings." This lightweight design makes the craft lethally agile, but leaves the pilot defenseless and unable to travel far from his base station. TIE pilots view shields as tools of cowards.

Emitter aperture

JAMMING UNIT

TIE FIGHTER FUELING PORT
TIE fighter fuel is a radioactive gas under high pressure. The twin ion engines of the ship have no moving parts, making the TIE easy to maintain.

DATA FILE

> Pilots rely on their self-contained flight suits to stay alive in space, as TIE fighters contain no life support systems.

> TIE fighters have no landing gear and are launched from special hangar racks.

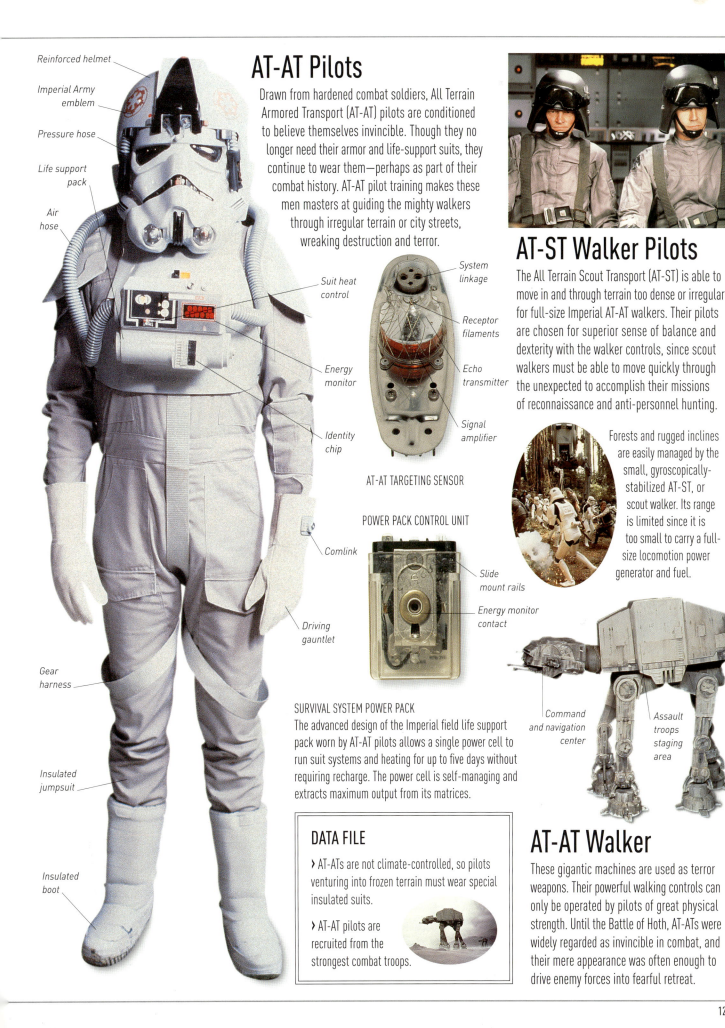

AT-AT Pilots

Drawn from hardened combat soldiers, All Terrain Armored Transport (AT-AT) pilots are conditioned to believe themselves invincible. Though they no longer need their armor and life-support suits, they continue to wear them—perhaps as part of their combat history. AT-AT pilot training makes these men masters at guiding the mighty walkers through irregular terrain or city streets, wreaking destruction and terror.

Reinforced helmet

Imperial Army emblem

Pressure hose

Life support pack

Air hose

Suit heat control

Energy monitor

Identity chip

Comlink

Driving gauntlet

Gear harness

Insulated jumpsuit

Insulated boot

System linkage

Receptor filaments

Echo transmitter

Signal amplifier

AT-AT TARGETING SENSOR

POWER PACK CONTROL UNIT

Slide mount rails

Energy monitor contact

SURVIVAL SYSTEM POWER PACK

The advanced design of the Imperial field life support pack worn by AT-AT pilots allows a single power cell to run suit systems and heating for up to five days without requiring recharge. The power cell is self-managing and extracts maximum output from its matrices.

AT-ST Walker Pilots

The All Terrain Scout Transport (AT-ST) is able to move in and through terrain too dense or irregular for full-size Imperial AT-AT walkers. Their pilots are chosen for superior sense of balance and dexterity with the walker controls, since scout walkers must be able to move quickly through the unexpected to accomplish their missions of reconnaissance and anti-personnel hunting.

Forests and rugged inclines are easily managed by the small, gyroscopically-stabilized AT-ST, or scout walker. Its range is limited since it is too small to carry a full-size locomotion power generator and fuel.

Command and navigation center

Assault troops staging area

DATA FILE

› AT-ATs are not climate-controlled, so pilots venturing into frozen terrain must wear special insulated suits.

› AT-AT pilots are recruited from the strongest combat troops.

AT-AT Walker

These gigantic machines are used as terror weapons. Their powerful walking controls can only be operated by pilots of great physical strength. Until the Battle of Hoth, AT-ATs were widely regarded as invincible in combat, and their mere appearance was often enough to drive enemy forces into fearful retreat.

Jabba the Hutt

AT THE CENTER of an extensive crime empire is the repellent crime lord Jabba the Hutt. Equipped with a cunning criminal mind, Jabba has built his syndicate through a long history of deals, threats, extortion, murders, and astute business arrangements. Unlike many of his competitors, Jabba is highly intelligent, and rarely overlooks details or dangers. Once bold and daring, he has settled back in his old age to a life of debauchery in his palace on Tatooine. Jabba enjoys violent entertainment almost as much as he enjoys profits, and he arranges deadly gladiatorial games and creative executions on a regular basis.

Jabba's palace is equipped with many security devices, including a semi-intelligent droid gatewatcher built into several of the entrances.

JABBA'S TATTOO, OF YORO ROOT PIGMENT

Telepath response unit

Brain support unit

Locomotion unit

Neurix tube

Spider leg

Detachable brain jar

Disembodied monk brain

Manipulator claw

B'OMARR MONK
Automated droid legs carry disembodied monks through the palace. The oldest spider droids have four legs, while more recent models have six.

Alkhara's Tower

Main citadel

Western Keep

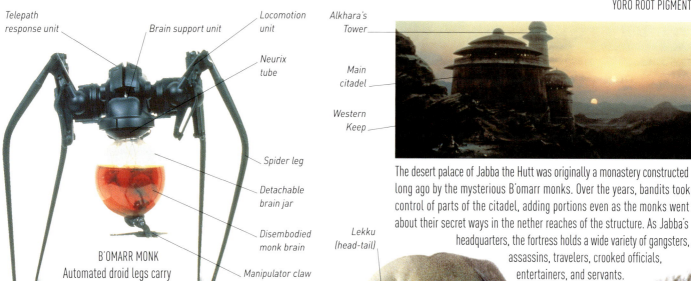

The desert palace of Jabba the Hutt was originally a monastery constructed long ago by the mysterious B'omarr monks. Over the years, bandits took control of parts of the citadel, adding portions even as the monks went about their secret ways in the nether reaches of the structure. As Jabba's headquarters, the fortress holds a wide variety of gangsters, assassins, travelers, crooked officials, entertainers, and servants.

Oola

Oola was kidnapped from a primitive clan by Jabba's majordomo Bib Fortuna, and trained by other Twi'lek girls in the art of seductive dance. Although Jabba finds her highly desirable, Oola refuses to give in to him.

Lekku (head-tail)

DATA FILE

> Jabba maintains a lavish estate in Mos Eisley, where he stays when conducting business at the spaceport. Wherever he is, he likes to eat nine meals a day.

> Although few suspect it, the creature called Buboicullaar, or Bubo, (right) is actually intelligent. He once ate a detonation link needed for a bomb, foiling an attempt to assassinate Jabba.

Jabba the Hutt

Jabba Desilijic Tiure, known to all as simply Jabba the Hutt, comes from the planet Nal Hutta, where he was raised (by his father, also a crime lord) to crave power and wealth. Hutts are notorious for their ruthless and amoral ways, and they often exploit their physical power to control weaker species. Hutts run most of the galaxy's large criminal syndicates.

Accompanied by lookouts on sand skiffs, Jabba's sail barge *Khetanna* carries the Hutt on journeys to Mos Eisley or to places of execution and gladiatorial combat staged for the crime lord's amusement.

Internal mantles shape a Hutt's head

Hutt skin secretes oil and mucus, making Hutts difficult to seize

Body has no skeleton

Muscular body can move like a snail or slither forward

Hookah pipe

Naal thorn burner

Hermi Odle

Ephant Mon

Jabba's palace is filled with bizarre creatures like his personal armorer, the Baragwin Hermi Odle. The former gun-runner Ephant Mon is Jabba's only real friend: the Hutt once saved his life.

Salacious Crumb

When Jabba first found this Kowakian monkey-lizard stealing his food, he tried to eat him, but later he became amused by the creature's antics. Salacious has since taken on the job of Jabba's court jester.

Salacious Crumb

Movable dais

The Sarlacc

SCIENTIFIC ANALYSIS has answered questions about many lifeforms in the galaxy, but some creatures continue to defy analysis, such as the Sarlacc. A rare, enormous beast, one Sarlacc rests in the basin of the Great Pit of Carkoon in the Northern Dune Sea on Tatooine. The Sarlacc's three-meter-wide mouth is the only part above ground level, and is otherwise completely concealed beneath the desert sands. While some xenobiologists argue over whether the Sarlacc is a plant or animal, most agree that the creature is far too dangerous to merit extended study.

The Sarlacc feeds on stray creatures that cannot escape the sandy slopes that surround its mouth, but not all of its meals are accidental. For many years, Jabba the Hutt delivered his enemies as "gifts" to the Sarlacc. Luke Skywalker was among the few to survive such a close encounter.

Jabba was surprised by the sudden, coordinated revolt of his Rebel captives. While the battle raged over the Great Pit of Carkoon, the Sarlacc simply waited for bodies to fall.

Touch-receptor tentacles

Inward-pointing teeth prevent victims from escaping

Rock-hard primary digestive glands

Tranquilizing poisons immobilize prey

Slower digestive route for more intellectually stimulating victims

Beaked tongue swallows small prey whole

Sand trap

Multiple hearts paired with multiple lungs

Site of Boba Fett's eventual escape

Moisture-gathering roots

Upper stabilizing limb senses movement in surrounding sands

Deadly Tongue

As the only visible aspect of the Sarlacc rests in the basin of the Great Pit of Carkoon, some mistakenly assume that the beak-tipped appendage at the basin's center is the creature's head. In fact, this eyeless protuberance is the Sarlacc's muscular tongue, which rises up from its mucous-lined mouth, seeking whatever savory morsels come its way.

Parasitic male remains attached to female for life

Unfortunate eopie

Anchored root system

Acidic juices dissolve soft membranes and digest smaller molecules of food

Careless anooba

The only known survivor of the Sarlacc's actual digestive system was Boba Fett, whose armored suit offered some protection from the creature as he used his weapons to blast his way out. It took years for Fett to recover from his wounds and regain his reputation.

Once swallowed, the Sarlacc's prey is incorporated into the biological system. It is believed that the Sarlacc absorbs the intellect of its victims, and is capable of sustaining their torment for thousands of years.

Still-sentient cocooned victims become part of the Sarlacc's collective intelligence

The Sarlacc claimed numerous lives during the skirmish that became known as the Battle of Carkoon, but many escaped the conflagration that consumed Jabba's sail barge. It remains unknown whether the Sarlacc prefers its meals live or roasted.

Transport tentacles place prey in specific areas of main stomach

Humanoid prey from one of Jabba's previous visits

Lower stabilizing limb

DATA FILE

> The Sarlacc is vulnerable to energy weapons, but most of its victims are unarmed. Those snared by the Sarlacc can only hope for rescue. Various factions have suggested that the Sarlacc should be destroyed, but more influential beings ensure its ongoing use as a most entertaining disposal system of their enemies.

Boba Fett

HAVING INHERITED JANGO FETT'S Mandalorian battle armor and arsenal of exotic weapons, Boba Fett assumes his father's mantle as a notorious and enigmatic bounty hunter. Over the years, Boba Fett has developed his own code of honor, and though he takes only certain assignments, he devotes himself to those few with fanatical skill. His cool and calculating ways combined with his manifold hidden capabilities have brought in many "impossible" marks, and earned his reputation as the best bounty hunter in the galaxy. From the concealed weapons covering his space suit to the disguised armaments of his starship *Slave I*, Boba Fett is unerringly a bounty's worst nightmare.

Boba Fett has worked for Darth Vader on several occasions, enough to have been called Vader's right-hand man. Vader finds Fett an intelligent, ruthless, capable ally, worthy to track Rebels and pursue Luke Skywalker.

Slave 1

Rotating cockpit capsule

Jango Fett had heavily modified his personal starship but Boba Fett continues to improve the aging craft. *Slave I* is jammed with weapons and customized tracking equipment of every kind, as well as a stolen military sensor masking system to hide him from those he stalks. Four on-board power generators are required to run the many weapons systems that can suddenly deploy from hidden panels.

Setting control

Organic alloy casing

HoloNet transmitter

S-thread detection matrix

Attachment magnet

Attachment frame

FALSE EYE (BACK)

Touchprint simulator surface

FALSE TOUCH

ION LIMPET HOMING BEACON

Jet Backpack

Missile

Fett's backpack is an excellent combination jumper-pack and rocket launcher. The launcher can be fitted with a missile or with a grappling hook projectile (attached to a rope and winch). The jet jumper system holds rocket blasts for short flights or for escaping and surprising Boba's prey.

Missile boost charge

Stabilizing gyro

Jet Pack adjustment tool

Missile launcher

Fuel tank

Missile targeting rangefinder

Directional servo

Activation button

Directional exhaust nozzles

Boba Fett uses these devices to track his marks and gain silent access to high security areas. A false touch pad clamps over touchprint locks to simulate the bioelectrical field and fingerprint of nearly any individual. A false eye pad can be applied to defeat retinal scan locks in a similar fashion. The ion limpet quietly uses the galactic HoloNet to track spacecraft throughout the known galaxy.

DATA FILE

> Fett is notorious for completely disintegrating those whom he has been hired to track down and kill.

> Working as a spy for Darth Vader, Boba Fett first encountered Luke Skywalker on a moon in the Panna system, where he almost tricked Luke into giving away the new location of the main Rebel base.

> Fett's services are famously expensive, but his honor cannot be bought. He only accepts missions which meet his harsh sense of justice.

Not even the Corellian smuggler Han Solo can escape the craft and determination of Boba Fett. Outsmarting all his bounty hunter rivals, Boba Fett tracks Solo to Bespin and there takes possession of his mark, loading Solo's carbon-frozen body into the cargo hold of *Slave I*.

Targeting rangefinder (retracted)

Targeting scope

EE-3 blaster rifle

Macrobinocular viewplate

Cooling vanes

Internal comlink allows Fett to summon Slave I from a distance

Motion/sound sensor system

Insulated gloves with armor mesh

Energized blast dissipation vest

Wrist gauntlet

Blast plates

Reinforced double-layered flight suit

Braided Wookiee scalps attest past hunts

Handgrip

Emitter

Activator

Weight-saving cutout

High-frequency screamer chip

Flanged Stibnium alloy blade

Power cell

Firing pin cover

Journeyman protector honor sash

Utility pouch

SURVIVAL KNIFE

SONIC BEAM WEAPON

KNEE PAD ROCKET DARTS

Kneepad rocket dart launchers

Having worked for the crime lord in the past as an enforcer, Boba Fett accepted a renewed assignment with Jabba the Hutt in return for a bonus added to the bounty on Han Solo. Some in Jabba's palace suspect that Fett also stayed on to admire his frozen trophy hanging in Jabba's throne room, but no one will ever know for sure.

Vibro-plate

Setting and intensity controls

Range marking

Concussion beam emitter

Satellite spin piercer

Trigger

Magno-thermitic charge

ANTI-SECURITY BLADES
Kept in Fett's shin pockets, these sophisticated electronic instruments can defeat fence fields and tune out security cameras and other alarm systems by the use of intense harmonic interference waves. Set higher, they can erase magnetic locks and give entry to nearly any door. Boba Fett uses them individually for most purposes, using several together to create a safe anti-security field for secret forced entries.

Boot spikes (spring-loaded)

Fragmentation housing

Ripper launch tip

Cycle wave ripper

For major demolition jobs, Boba Fett is known to use an antiquated multi-detonator, less susceptible to damper shield effects than a conventional thermal detonator, and capable of tearing a starship engine into fragments.

MULTI-DETONATOR

Ewoks

DEEP WITHIN the primeval forests of the emerald moon of Endor, the small, furry Ewoks live in harmony with the natural world around them. They build their villages high in the oldest trees, connecting their dwellings with wooden bridges and suspended platforms. Ewoks hunt and gather by day on the forest floor, retreating to their aerial villages by night, when the forest becomes too dangerous for them.

Sounding sticks

Retaining strap

Leather strap

Handle

Stone knife

HUNTING KNIFE

Sheath

CHURI BIRD CALLERS

Hood

Spear

Thick fur

Stone club head

Authority stick

Gurreck skull headress

Churi feathers

Striped pelt

Teebo

A watcher of the stars and a poet at heart, Teebo has a mystical alignment with the forces of nature. His subtle perception lets him see more than meets his dreamer's eye, but he is also a practical thinker. His sound judgment has led to his position as a leader within his tribe.

Thickened head lends weight to blows

FIGHTING CLUBS

Wicket W. Warrick

A young loner, Wicket is off traveling when he encounters Princess Leia Organa in the forest. Helping her to the relative safety of his village, he comes to trust her and senses her goodness of spirit. When Leia's friends arrive, Wicket argues that they should be spared any abuse, but his solitary habits leave him with small influence amongst the village elders. Wicket's thorough knowledge of the forest terrain greatly assists the Rebels in their later attack on the Imperial forces.

An Ewok shaman builds a collection of many magical objects and medicinal cures for his work. A spirit staff helps summon dead ancestors for assistance, while the sick or injured are touched with a powerful healing wand. The forest vegetation offers many medicinal plants, which are kept with charms in a talisman bag.

Talisman bag

Healing wand

SHAMAN'S KIT

SHAMAN'S GHOST RATTLE

Logray

A tribal shaman and medicine man, Logray uses his knowledge of ritual and magic to help and awe his people. He still favors the old traditions of initiation and live sacrifice. The trophies on his staff of power include the remnants of old enemies. Logray is suspicious of all outsiders, an attitude reinforced by the arrival of Imperial forces.

Churi skull

Staff of power

Trophy spine

Chief Chirpa

Leader of his tribe for 42 seasons, Chief Chirpa has the wisdom of long years. He leads his people with understanding, even though he has become a bit forgetful in his old age. His authority commits the Ewoks to their dangerous fight against the Empire.

Hood

Hunting knife

Chief's medallion

Medicine bag

Striped fur

DATA FILE

› Their technology may be primitive, but the Ewoks display resourceful ingenuity, constructing hang gliders and complex traps for Imperial occupation forces.

› Ewoks often wear the teeth, horns, and skulls of animals they have hunted as trophies.

The Cantina Crowd

THE MOS EISLEY SPACEPORT sees a wide variety of unusual people and things, but the Mos Eisley Cantina is known as the haunt of the weirdest clientele in town. Hardened professional spacers and bizarre outlanders from distant corners of the galaxy can be found here. It's no place for the squeamish, but for its regulars, the cantina provides a pan-galactic atmosphere that helps distract them from their various misfortunes and the miserable hole of Mos Eisley. The regular band suits many tastes, and as long as foolish outsiders don't step in and get their heads blown off, everyone can have their own version of a good time. Deals get made, things get drunk, and the wrong sorts of business go the right sorts of ways. The bartender maintains a semblance of order by threatening to poison the drinks of creatures that give him trouble.

An entrance vestibule serves as a buffer between the intolerable heat outdoors and the relative cool inside the cantina. It also gives those inside an opportunity to look over new arrivals before they step in.

Seats for waiting

Droid detector

Drink cups indicate cantina's services

Hrchek Kal Fas is a tough Saurin droid trader who wisely keeps his bodyguard nearby in the cantina.

Duros are a species long adapted to space travel, with natural piloting and navigation skills. These two make regular deep space runs connecting through Mos Eisley.

Distinctive Devaronian horns

This Devaronian hides under the assumed name of Labria, on the run from a wicked past and one of the galaxy's highest bounties for his deadly crimes.

Ommni wheel

Mouthpiece

Farra slots

FANFAR

OMMNI BOX

Sound projector

Power unit

Support post

Bwom pedal

Thwee pedal

TECH M'OR   TEDN DAHAI

DATA FILE

> When Luke and Ben left the cantina they did not realize that they were spotted by the insect-eating Garindan, a low-life informant carrying an Imperial comlink.

> Bodies or severed limbs from altercations in the cantina never seem to be there when the authorities show up... no one is quite sure what happens to them.

Living beneath Mos Eisley in abandoned tunnels, this Talz named Muftak works as a pickpocket. Talz are a primitive species who use few tools, and are taken into space only by slavers.

Day vision eyes (night vision eyes beneath)

The cantina's diverse selection of legal and illegal drinks draws unusual visitors. Lamproids and other marginal species are served blood mixes that are of questionable origin.

Figrin D'an and his Band

The Bith musicians most often heard in the cantina are highly intelligent creatures with sophisticated musical abilities—a band called the Modal Nodes. Even though they complain, the band members enjoy their out-of-the-way dive and are glad to be away from their home world of Clak'dor VII. The lead player is an expert gambler who lives well and pays off his occasional debts with his tunes, and meanwhile tries to keep his members out of trouble. They've been asked to play at Jabba's palace, but they're too smart for that.

Mouth tube

KLOO HORN

Tone mode selectors

Enlarged cranium

Large eyes

Respiratory folds

Reciprocator horns

Ploong sounder

Peel rods

Band pants

Travel boots

FIGRIN D'AN

BANDFILL

Band jacket

Power indicator

NALAN CHEEL

FIZZZ (OR DORENIAN BESHNIQUEL)

Peel rod

DOIKK NA'TS

137

Creatures

The ghastly toothed sand creatures of Tatooine's deep deserts can grow to over 100 meters in length.

COUNTLESS VARIETIES of life forms inhabit the galaxy, many known only to those who have encountered them and myriads unclassified by galactic science. Long after dark, space pilots may trade tales over drinks about weird and horrible creatures on remote planets or in the far reaches of space. More than once these stories have turned out to be true, from the haunting howls of Hoth's stalking snow beast to the impossibly gigantic asteroid lurkers, closing their maws on fleeing starships. The doubtful traveler is often the last one to realize that a tentacle is already curled around his leg, about to draw him to some unspeakable death. In a galaxy full of creatures such as these, it pays to be careful.

Space Slug

Silicon-based space slugs survive in a vacuum, digesting minerals with a uranium-based metabolism. Recently a titan space slug was documented by an Imperial Star Destroyer on a pursuit mission in an asteroid field. The slug attacked and digested part of the Imperial vessel before being subdued.

Dianoga

Dianogas (or garbage squids) have spread throughout the galaxy, growing up to ten meters long and thriving especially in sewers. Feeding on refuse, these creatures are sometimes bred in space stations for waste processing. Older specimens are very aggressive, seizing prey in their seven muscular tentacles.

Space-living silicon-based parasites, mynocks attack the signal emitters and power cables of starships, feeding on the energy emissions. They can cause significant damage to ships they infest.

Mild-tempered rontos are used by settled Jawa clans on Tatooine as pack animals, bringing goods to cities for trade.

Tauntaun bones

Curving horns

Fanged maw

Camouflaging white pelt

Thick insulating fur

The worrt inhabits the wastelands of Tatooine, attacking almost any moving object. Jabba keeps worrts in the grounds outside his palace.

Manacles

Wampa

Standing three meters high, huge wampa ice creatures hunt tauntauns and other creatures on the snow plains of Hoth, where their howling wails blend with the icy winds at night. Cunning predators, wampas are normally solitary beasts, but they have been known to band together with uncanny intelligence in the face of threats like human settlements.

The rock wart of Tatooine uses a painful neurotoxic venom in its bite and sting to kill even large prey.

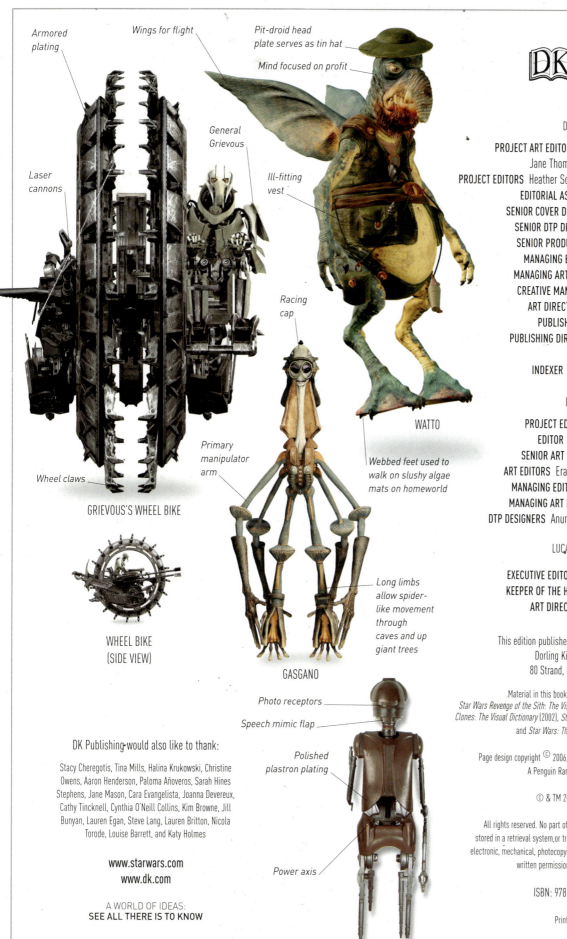

Armored plating

Wings for flight

Pit-droid head plate serves as tin hat

Mind focused on profit

Laser cannons

General Grievous

Ill-fitting vest

Racing cap

Wheel claws

GRIEVOUS'S WHEEL BIKE

Primary manipulator arm

Webbed feet used to walk on slushy algae mats on homeworld

WATTO

WHEEL BIKE (SIDE VIEW)

Long limbs allow spider-like movement through caves and up giant trees

GASGANO

Photo receptors

Speech mimic flap

Polished plastron plating

Power axis

EV-9D9

DK | Penguin Random House

DK LONDON

PROJECT ART EDITORS Dan Bunyan, Nick Avery, Jane Thomas and Iain Morris
PROJECT EDITORS Heather Scott, Laura Gilbert and David Pickering
EDITORIAL ASSISTANT Matt Jones
SENIOR COVER DESIGNER Mark Penfound
SENIOR DTP DESIGNER Kavita Varma
SENIOR PRODUCER Charlotte Oliver
MANAGING EDITOR Sadie Smith
MANAGING ART EDITOR Ron Stobbart
CREATIVE MANAGER Sarah Harland
ART DIRECTOR Lisa Lanzarini
PUBLISHER Julie Ferris
PUBLISHING DIRECTOR Simon Beecroft

INDEXER Marian Anderson

DK INDIA

PROJECT EDITOR Samira Sood
EDITOR Pragati Nagpal
SENIOR ART EDITOR Neha Ahuja
ART EDITORS Era Chawla and Rohit Walia
MANAGING EDITOR Glenda Fernandes
MANAGING ART EDITOR Navidita Thapa
DTP DESIGNERS Anurag Trivedi and Manish Upreti

LUCASFILM LTD.

EXECUTIVE EDITOR Jonathan W. Rinzler
KEEPER OF THE HOLOCRON Leland Chee
ART DIRECTOR Troy Alders

This edition published in Great Britain in 2015 by
Dorling Kindersley Limited
80 Strand, London WC2R 0RL

Material in this book was previously published in:
Star Wars Revenge of the Sith: The Visual Dictionary (2005), *Star Wars Attack of the Clones: The Visual Dictionary* (2002), *Star Wars Episode I: The Visual Dictionary* (1999) and *Star Wars: The Visual Dictionary* (1998)

Page design copyright © 2006, 2012, 2015 Dorling Kindersley Limited
A Penguin Random House Company

© & TM 2015 Lucasfilm Ltd.

All rights reserved. No part of this publication may be reproduced, stored in a retrieval system, or transmitted in any form or by any means, electronic, mechanical, photocopying, recording, or otherwise, without prior written permission of the copyright owner.

ISBN: 978-0-2412-1716-0

Printed in Italy.

DK Publishing would also like to thank:

Stacy Cheregotis, Tina Mills, Halina Krukowski, Christine Owens, Aaron Henderson, Paloma Añoveros, Sarah Hines Stephens, Jane Mason, Cara Evangelista, Joanna Devereux, Cathy Tincknell, Cynthia O'Neill Collins, Kim Browne, Jill Bunyan, Lauren Egan, Steve Lang, Lauren Britton, Nicola Torode, Louise Barrett, and Katy Holmes

www.starwars.com
www.dk.com

A WORLD OF IDEAS:
SEE ALL THERE IS TO KNOW

LANDSPEEDER A repulsorlift vehicle used for traveling at low altitude over land.

LASER CANNON Often mounted on a ship or vehicle, this weapon shoots visible bolts of coherent light in a rapid-fire fashion. More powerful than a blaster.

LIGHTSABER The elegant weapon of the Jedi, lightsabers are swords with blades of pure energy that can cut through nearly any object. They can also be used to deflect fired energy bolts.

MIDI-CHLORIANS Microscopic organisms that exist in all living things, and can be detected and measured by a simple analysis of blood or other genetic material. Especially abundant in Force-sensitive beings, midi-chlorians allow Jedi and Sith to tap into the Force.

MOFF Title given to Imperial military commanders who ruled certain sectors of the galaxy, and who reported to Grand Moffs.

NAV COMPUTER Sometimes called a navicomputer, a nav computer is a specialized processing unit used to calculate lightspeed jumps and routes and trajectories through hyperspace and realspace.

OUTER RIM TERRITORIES A group of star systems that lie beyond the Core worlds.

PHOTORECEPTOR A device that captures light rays and converts them into electronic signals for processing by video computers. Photoreceptors are used as eyes in most droids.

PODRACER Essentially a control pod linked to two large repulsorlift engines, Podracers are high-speed vehicles used in professional racing tournaments. Podracer pilots are also called Podracers.

PROTON TORPEDO A projectile weapon that carries a proton-scattering warhead. Proton torpedoes can be fired from starfighters or shoulder-mounted launchers.

REBEL ALLIANCE The common term used for the Alliance to Restore the Republic, which rebelled against Palpatine's Galactic Empire.

REPUBLIC The common term used for the Galactic Republic, the united worlds of the galaxy, which eventually fell to the Galactic Empire.

REPULSORLIFT An engine that employs an antigravitational propulsion unit called a repulsor, repulsorlifts provide thrust for landspeeders and airspeeders, and are also used in small starships for docking and atmospheric flight.

SANDCRAWLER Engineered as ore haulers and mobile refineries, sandcrawlers are enormous vehicles that travel on treads. Abandoned sandcrawlers are typically salvaged for use by indigenous beings.

SEPARATISTS Initially a political movement by those who sought to break their alliance with the Galactic Republic, the Separatists officially united as the Confederacy.

SITH An ancient sect of Force-sensitive beings, the secretive Sith use their powers for evil. Their goal is to destroy the Jedi and conquer the galaxy.

SPICE A name given to a variety of drugs, including the glitterstim spice mined underground on the planet Kessel.

STARFIGHTER A combat starship, typically operated by a single pilot.

THERMAL DETONATOR A powerful hand-size bomb that disintegrates everything in its 20-meter blast radius.

TIBANNA GAS A rare gas that can produce greater energy yield in blasters. Tibanna gas is frozen in carbonite for export from refineries.

TRACTOR BEAM A modified force field that can immobilize and move objects. Tractor beams are generally used in spaceports to guide ships to safe landings, but can also be used to capture ships.

TRADE FEDERATION The commerce faction controlled by the Neimoidians, the Confederacy-allied Trade Federation was the largest commercial corporation in the galaxy.

CUT-AWAY STORMTROOPER HELMET

Holographic memory cell

RATH RECORDER

Wupiupi pouch

TATOOINE MONEY BELT

Sunshield roll

Condensing canteens

DESERT SURVIVAL BACKPACK

HITMAN'S BLASTER

Flashy decor

Burnished alloy shell

NABOO DETONATOR

SITH TRACER BEACON

Key Terms

ACADEMY Training institution for Exploration, Military, and Merchant Services.

AIRSPEEDER Repulsorlift-powered vehicle designed to operate inside a planet's protective atmosphere. Some airspeeders can soar more than 250 kilometers high at a speed of more than 900 kilometers an hour. Models include the T-16 skyhopper and Rebel-modified snowspeeders.

ASTROMECH All-around utility droids that carry out computer repairs and undertake information retrieval. Usually short, cylindrical, and tripedal, astromech droids specialize in starship maintenance and repair.

BLASTER Commonly used energy weapons, blasters have adjustable settings to fire beams of intense light that can stun, kill, or vaporize. Models range from handheld blaster pistols and rifles to large blaster cannons that require a crew to operate.

BOUNTY HUNTER Individuals who hunt criminals, outlaws, and predatory creatures for a reward. The Bounty Hunters' Guild upholds their creed, which states that no hunter can kill another hunter or interfere with another's hunt.

CARBONITE A strong but highly volatile metal used to preserve materials such as Tibanna gas, which is frozen in carbonite to allow long-distance transport.

CLONE WARS The interstellar battle fought between the Galactic Republic (which employed clone soldiers under the command of Jedi generals) and the Confederacy of Independent Systems.

COMLINK A personal communications transceiver that consists of a transmitter, receiver, and power source.

CONFEDERACY The common term used for the Confederacy of Independent Systems, an alliance of interstellar commerce factions committed to capitalism and the eventual abolition of all trade barriers.

CORE WORLDS Prestigious and densely populated, the Core Worlds border the central area of the galaxy, and were allied with the Republic before the rise of the Empire.

CREDITS Basic monetary unit used throughout the galaxy.

CYBORG A cybernetic organism, combining technological and organic parts.

DEATH STAR An Imperial moon-sized battle station, equipped with a planet-destroying superlaser.

EMPIRE The common term used for the Republic of the Galactic Empire, ruled by Emperor Palpatine.

ESCAPE POD A technological lifeboat, used by passengers and crew to abandon starships.

THE FORCE An energy field generated by all living things, and which binds the entire galaxy.

HOLOCRON Device used to store and access information for Force-sensitive beings.

HOLOGRAM Three-dimensional image constructed from waves of light. Used for recordings and communications.

HOLONET Interstellar network that allows hologramic communication throughout the galaxy.

HYPERSPACE A dimension of space-time that can be reached only by traveling beyond light-speed velocity.

ION CANNON A weapon that fires bursts of ionized energy to damage mechanical and computer systems without causing structural damage.

JEDI Originally protectors of the Republic, Jedi are sensitive to the Force and able to manipulate its energies to help and serve others.

GRAND MOFF TARKIN'S CODE CYLINDER

Activator

ADMIRAL MOTTI'S CODE CYLINDERS

Temperature control unit

Neck seal

STORMTROOPER SERGEANT'S PAULDRON

Fastener

Retainer clip

Comlink

Power unit

Auxiliary equipment port

STORMTROOPER GRAPPLING HOOK

REBEL HOTH BACKPACK

Black rank pad

ENLISTED STORMTROOPER'S PAULDRON

Rotating shoulder bearing

Motor and gear drive

Brooks Propulsion rocket boosters

Turbine

All-terrain tread

Fuel distribution manifold with quick-disconnects

Post-warranty BPD rocket thruster

Explosion-proof durasteel shell

Everett Mark IV Locomotion System

Fuel regulator

Kevdan Aerosystems hydro-glycolic fuel cells

Quick release latching mechanism

Fuel assembly slides out for maintenance and replacement

Electro magnetic power charge arm

Gear rotates arm into position

Servomotor to deploy devices

Data linkage port and console opens to deploy more devices

UTILITY ARM CAROUSEL

To economize space within an astromech's cylindrical torso, interchangeable arms are fitted onto rotating carousels. This assembly allows R2 to quickly deploy a specific arm, creating an illusion of an endless variety of concealed tools.

DATA FILE

> C-3PO is less resilient than R2-D2 requiring frequent repairs and maintenance. Fortunately, R2 can do repairs almost as fast as he can cycle through his tools.

GROUNDED ASTROMECH

Brooks Propulsion Devices (BPD), which manufactured rocket thrusters for astromechs, was shut down by the Empire after the Clone Wars. R2-D2 eventually damaged his BPD components, but has only occasionally regretted the loss of his flying ability.

R2-D2 Expanded

VARIOUS OWNER MODIFICATIONS and sometime limited availability of non-standard optional features gives older model Industrial Automaton astromech droids a reputation for being laden with improvised, exotic, and obsolete assemblies. Although infrequent memory wipes can instill idiosyncratic behavior in most intelligent droids, aged astromechs such as R2-D2 are known for extreme quirkiness. Despite loyalty to his allies, R2 is notoriously good at keeping secrets and is not quick to reveal all of his technological capabilities.

Holographic Projector

By accessing data, R2-D2 can create three-dimensional holographic displays of starship systems. To make a holographic recording of a proximal being or object, the droid's visual sensors are used in combination with his acoustic signaler; an automatic analysis of reflected sound waves creates a visual pattern that "fills in" the areas that R2 cannot see directly.

Gimbal provides tilt adjustment

Nethal Industries RGB photoreceptor lenses

Stears Data multifunction optical readers

Electromagnetic field sensor unit

Protective lens and filter

Extendible auxiliary visual imaging system

RECORDED MEMORIES
By sacrificing some free memory, R2 retains several holographic recordings in his system, including Princess Leia's desperate plea for help from Obi-Wan Kenobi and other messages that he regards as historically or personally significant.

Four-way servomotor control

VicksVisc holo-casing

Kerner optical holo emitter

Fiber-optic data cable

EXTENDIBLE NECK
Equipped with an extendible neck to allow his insertion into the droid socket of a Naboo N-1 starfighter, R2-D2 has long ignored this particular feature of his assembly, as its use generally invites unwelcome particles into his systems.

Extendable fire extinguisher

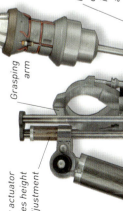
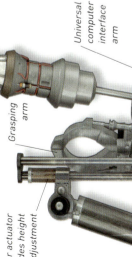
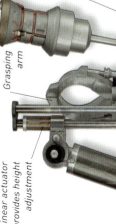
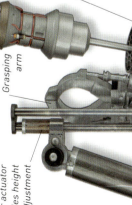

Commutator

Power distribution umbilical

Coupling for power distribution

Head rotation servomotor

Hydraulic head extenders

Protective casing

Data cable bus

DROID LOGIC
R2 lacks the intuitive and associative capabilities of many organic species, but his unique experiences, observations, and memories have distinctly affected his highly developed logic circuits. He is unusually innovative and decisive.

Imaharatronics logic display sensors

Universal computer interface arm

Grasping arm

Linear actuator provides height adjustment

Rancor Monster

Standing five meters tall, this fearsome carnivore possesses an armored skin and colossal strength. Jabba keeps this beast in a pit beneath one of his palace courts, feeding it a live diet of unfortunate victims and watching its attacks for amusement. Jabba keeps the origin of his bizarre, freakish pet a mystery, though there are little-known legends of rancor-like monsters on the remote planet of Dathomir.

DATA FILE

› Dianogas change color to match their last meal, turning translucent if they have not eaten for a long time.

› Jabba's pet Hoover (below) looks harmless, but creeps up on sleeping victims to suck their blood at night, using its nose trunk to slither through clothing or around blankets.

The animal handler Malakili became an outlaw when some of his circus beasts escaped during a show and killed much of the audience. Jabba then hired him as keeper of the murderous rancor, which Malakili has grown fond of.

Powerful jaw muscles

Digestive spittle

Long reaching arms

Claws

Wide grasp

Gaffi stick; gift from some Tusken Raiders for killing a giant mutant womp rat that took over their clan cave

Clutching fingers

Old circus pants

Short legs

Tough, rigid hide can absorb blaster bolts

Stubby hooves

Rancors are inherently benign and have been domesticated by the Witches of Dathomir, but Jabba takes every measure to encourage ferocious behavior in his own rancor. Consumed by rage and hunger, Jabba's rancor proved immune to Luke Skywalker's persuasive Jedi mind tricks when they battled in the creature's pit.